Common spaces of urban emancipation

MANCHESTER
1824

Manchester University Press

Common spaces of urban emancipation

STAVROS STAVRIDES

Manchester University Press

Published by Manchester University Press
Altrincham Street, Manchester M1 7JA

www.manchesteruniversitypress.co.uk

British Library Cataloguing-in-Publication Data
A catalogue record for this book is available from the British Library

ISBN   978 1 5261 3559 9   hardback
ISBN   978 1 5261 3560 5   paperback

First published 2019

Typeset in Minion by
Servis Filmsetting Ltd, Stockport, Cheshire

To Evgenia and Zoe.

Contents

Figures

All images are the property of the author, except where noted.

Introduction and acknowledgements

This book explores contemporary urban experiences connected to practices of sharing and collaboration. Becoming part of a growing discussion on the cultural meaning and the politics of urban commons, it uses examples from Europe and Latin America to support the view that a world of mutual support and urban solidarity emerges today in, against, and beyond existing societies of inequality. In such a world, people experience the potentialities of emancipation activated by concrete forms of space commoning.

In the everydayness of self-organized neighborhoods, in the struggles for justice in occupied public spaces, in the emergence of "territories in resistance" (Zibechi 2012), and in dissident artistic practices of collaborative creation, collective inventiveness produces fragments of a better future.

Entering the discussion on the political meaning of struggles to preserve and expand "the commons" (De Angelis 2007 and 2017, Hardt and Negri 2009, Harvey 2012, De Angelis and Stavrides 2010, Stavrides 2016) in a world of enclosures and exploitation of human collaboration, this book traces the ways space production shapes such struggles. Concrete collective experiences of urban space appropriation and participatory design experiments indicate differing but potentially compatible trajectories through which common space (or space-as-commons) becomes an important factor in social change. In space commoning we can trace elements of a different, emancipating future, new ideas about social organization, and new patterns of collective experiences through which people actively shape such a future in and through inhabited spaces.

Thinking about social emancipation needs to be firmly grounded in the rich realities of struggle and counter-dominant ways of organizing social life that today produce alternatives to the existing geometries of power. This is why this book was developed through a careful participatory study of such emerging realities in different social contexts. This is an effort that by no means claims to be based on an exhaustive survey of relevant events throughout the world. However, the examples analyzed can be taken to be indicative of contemporary possibilities unfolding in a moment of globally interconnected dissident experiences.

Usually case studies are treated as areas of research in which major theoretical constructions are being tested. I strongly believe that theory needs to be produced by carefully learning from what people actually do and from what reflections they produce while challenging established dogmas by their actions. Thus, basing an argument on the words and ideas of established thinkers necessarily needs to be complemented (or questioned) by attentive reappraisals of the words and ideas of less distinguished or so-called "anonymous" people. Collective inventiveness is a major source of inspiration for this book. And a deep respect for all those people who contribute to such collective forms of creativity in search for a more just world seems to be a major motivating force behind it.

Part of the book includes interviews with crucial informants relating to each case being analyzed: Zeyno Perkunlu, a member of an activist group involved in the Istanbul Gezi Park occupation, in chapter 4; Stefano Portelli, a community activist of Bon Pastor struggle, in chapter 5; Pedro Arantes, an activist professor member of the USINA team, in chapter 6; Gerardo Meza and Sergio Pacheco, leading activists in the corresponding autonomous neighborhoods in Mexico, in chapter 7; and Aimée Zito Lema, the artist who conceived the project "Sitting is a Verb," in chapter 8. I am deeply indebted to them for their contribution. I am also thankful to Benjamin Nahum (FUCVAM), Germano Wagner (USINA), and Joviano Meier

(Brigadas Populares, Belo Horizonte, Brazil) for their interviews, which crucially contributed to the development of the research material and arguments of this book. If emancipatory commoning necessarily includes and promotes many different voices, it is important to trace the way they articulate their views and to be able to follow their reasoning rather than only translating them to a general idea.

The arguments developed here were tested and reworked in the context of both academic and activist environments. It would be impossible to thank each and every one of those who have contributed to the grounding and elaboration of the ideas that unfold in this work. Among them, the students in the undergraduate and postgraduate courses I teach at NTUA have for many years been both my relentless critics and my valuable collaborators.

I feel that I should especially thank some of those whose criticism and remarks in differing discussion contexts have enriched my arguments and helped me in clarifying my theoretical scopes: Markus Bader, Joanna Braga, Yves Cabannes, Oriol Nel·lo Colom, Massimo De Angelis, Lieven De Cauter, Gustavo Esteva, Begüm Özden Firat, Pascal Gielen, Mathias Heyden, John Holloway, Michael Janoschka, Maria Kopanari, Penny Koutrolikou, Socratis Stratis, Alessio Surian, Charis Tsavdaroglou, Carlos Vainer, and Raul Zibechi.

Special thanks to Thomas Dark of Manchester University Press, who has supported the book's publishing in a very encouraging, as well as efficient, way.

Evgenia Michalopoulou and Zoe Stavrides Michalopoulou have been, as always, inspiring, supportive, and ready to criticize any of my theoretical arguments that appear to be attracted by academic elitism! They both know very well what I owe to them.

An earlier version of part of chapter 1 was published in N. Dockx and G. Pascal (eds) (2018), *Exploring Commonism: A New Aesthetics of the Real* (Amsterdam: Valiz) under the title 'The potentials of space commoning.'

Chapter 2 is a greatly reworked and extended version of the published text 'Toward an architecture of commoning,' *ASAP/ Journal*, vol. 1/1 (2016), 77–94

Chapter 3 includes parts of the text 'Practising self-government:

space matters,' published in *Naked Punch*, special issue 19/2017, 12–16.

Chapter 4 includes parts of my contribution to the article: A. Fernández-Savater and C. Flesher Fominaya (eds), with contributions by Luhuna Carvalho, Çiğdem, Hoda Elsadda, Wiam El-Tamami, Patricia Horrillo, Silvia Nanclares & Stavros Stavrides (2017) 'Life after the squares: reflections on the consequences of the Occupy movements,' *Social Movement Studies*, 16/1, 119–151.

Chapter 5 includes parts of the text 'Reinventing social housing?,' in Col.Lectiu Repensar Bonpastor (eds) (2016), *Repensar Bonpastor: Teijendo historias urbanas de Barcelona desde el umbral de las Casas Baratas* (Barcelona: Col.Lectiu Repensar Bonpastor), 453–454.

Chapter 6 includes a small part of my published text 'Toward an architecture of commoning,' *ASAP/Journal*, vol. 1/1 (2016), 77–94.

Chapter 7 includes parts of the text 'Common space: Die Stadt als Gemeingut. Eine Einfuehrung,' in S. Stavrides and M. Heyden (2016), *Gemeingut Stadt* (Berlin: neue Gesellschaft fuer bildende Kunst), 14–60.

1

Space as potential

Commoning experience

What this work attempts to establish is a rethinking of the possibility of human emancipation through a rethinking of space: space considered both as a concrete social reality (city, house, public space, territory) and as a form, a pattern, which is employed, along with other forms, to establish and reproduce the contested meanings of social reality. Space is considered both the locus of experience and a powerful means for constructing thoughts on and representations of what exists. In terms of experience, space concretizes relations between actually existing people ("singularities" according to Paolo Virno – we will return to this), which shape the horizon of the sensible. What Jacques Rancière actually suggests is that the "distribution of the sensible" is a socially regulated process which does not simply dominate thought (as in the ideological dressage established by relevant ideological apparatuses) but, crucially, experience, what is to be experienced. Experience may become a social fact only when it is shared, only when it is represented (expressed, narrated, shown through voluntary or involuntary body signs as, for example, in an exclamation or in a cry of anguish). Experience, then, is socially controlled through the distribution of the sensible because it is made a social fact through exchanges of actions and expressions between people. Although the distribution of the sensible tries to limit and arrange the field of possible experiences and thus cripple experience as potentiality, the social life of experiences is a process of sharing, which in principle may escape dominant classifications.

The reasons for this are of two different kinds. The first kind is ontological, as it refers to the very character of the human species. As Virno suggests: "Our species is characterized by its 'openness to the world' – if we understand by 'world' a vital context which is always unpredictable and partially undetermined" (2009: 98). Openness, according to this view, is caused by the lack of precise instincts and drives which would univocally guide the human animal to construct its habitat.

The second kind of reason is partially the product of the first one. Because the human species is open to the world, it develops a multiplicity of "solutions" to its survival, based on the construction of different forms of social organization. History, then, considered as the temporal canvas on which those differentiations may be projected, essentially opens the field of potential experiences. Different epochs have constructed and de-constructed different patterns of the sensible. The sensible, thus, constitutes a contested terrain, importantly linked to the production and reproduction of a certain social organization.

Virno suggests that this species-specific openness to the world goes hand in hand with a predominant pre-individual reality that precedes the process of individuation. The human individual retains the pre-individual traits of the species (2015b: 224), which are the generic human faculties (language being the most important of them), and is being constructed historically as a singular subject in the context of a specific society.

This approach puts at the very center of the problematization of the common the idea that the process of individuation follows an ambiguous and probably contradictory path, which starts from a condition of commonness: "What is unique, unrepeatable, fragile, comes from what is undifferentiated and generic" (2015b: 224).

On the importance of this pre-individual reality, Virno summons important, albeit diverse, thinkers. Among them are G. Simondon, who identifies the pre-individual reality with nature; M. Merleau Ponty, who considers sensations as anterior and alien to personal life (2015b: 225); and Vygotsky, who insists on the "pre-individual, immediately social nature of human speech" (2015b: 226). What is, however, the cornerstone according to Virno of this pre-individual reality is thought, the shared capacity to think, which is historically mobilized in different societies as shared knowledge and ways to knowledge, a condition that Marx has termed "general intellect" (2015b: 227). What is common to all humans, then, according to this approach, precedes the processes of differentiation which result in historically distinct individuals (and individual trajectories).

A different approach to human ontogenesis also discovers and supports the primacy of the common as compared to individual. One phrase that emblematizes it in J. L. Nancy's words is: "Being is in common" (1991: 1). Commonness is not something which can be separated from existence. "Being cannot *be* anything but being-with-one-another, circulating in the *with* and as the *with* of this singularly plural coexistence" (2000: 3, emphasis in original).

For Nancy, the ontological primacy of the common does not refer to a generic level of human capacities but it clearly describes the necessary foundation of sense: "any sense is necessarily *common sense* … with the meaning that any sense is made of communication, of sharing or exchange" (2010: 150, emphasis in original). Singularities exist and are shaped within a shared horizon of being, and they cannot be subtracted from such an inclusive horizon. So, if there are processes of differentiation between and of individuals, these are integral to the essence of being. Being is common, it is being with, it is being singular because of the plurality developed within this "with."

That is why Nancy openly confronts identitarian policies and discourses on purity (of race, of culture etc.), which essentially cancel the foundational role of the "with." In his "Eulogy for the meleé" (2000) and with direct reference to the nationalist purisms which destroyed Sarajevo (the city of *meleé* par excellence) he states: "The common, having-in-common or being-in-common, excludes interior unity, subsistence and presence in and for itself" (2010: 154). Pure "uncontaminated" identity, pure originary identity enclosed in its solipsistic self-affirmation, is really a fantasy. It can become, however, a very dangerous fantasy, a lethal one.

Returning to the problematization of space and its relation to human emancipation, we may suggest that the inherent dynamics of the experience (ontologically and historically potentially open to non-predetermined patterns) makes concrete spatial conditions both the means for and the scope of upsetting any historically dominant "distribution of the sensible." An obvious way in which unclassified or even "dissident" experiences may arise is by making visible what was not before (and this does not necessarily mean that what was not visible did not exist – making visible means directing experience towards something that becomes, thus, socially meaningful). Spatial arrangements may be obviously used to hide, to reveal, to exalt, and to compare in terms of visible characteristics. Spaces may be concretely employed in producing, enhancing, or destroying visibility (of acts, actors, objects etc.). If emancipation has to do with social relations that are based on equality, justice, sharing, and solidarity, experiences in space, experiences shaped through existing spaces, may concretize such relations in the form of lived conditions. And what is more, the actual unfolding of such relations in space may become the testing ground for their emancipatory potential.

Struggles and representations

Sharing experiences does not simply mean being part of the same event, being "there" and "then" together with others. If experience is not only an individual processing of outer stimuli but a complex form of interaction with human and non-human environment, one needs to dwell on the intricacies of such a process: interaction, when focused especially on humans, has to do with voluntary and involuntary ways of responding to the actions of others. Experience, thus, is shaped in action and is expressed as action. Exchanges employ a whole array of means in which experiences are shared by being expressed and actually unfold by being expressed. In the context of human society, experience is socialized and socialization develops in time and "takes place" in space through shared experiences.

It seems that one of the most important ways in which the sharing of experiences happens is based on space considered as a form. Referring to spatial forms, people may convey experiences of protected life or horrified uncertainty in front of an unfathomable unknown, depending of course on the context of experiences and the conditions of sharing. Experience becomes meaningful but it is actually transformed in the process of becoming meaningful according to the socio-historical framework of sharing. Available spatial forms (presented through stereotypical images, diagrams, photographic snapshots, etc.) are not to be reduced to inert containers which give recognizable form to experience considered as the formless raw material produced by the senses. Available spatial forms, developed through social education, actually interact with experiences while giving them form. Spatial forms in such a context are more like dynamic constellations of spatial relations concertized by being employed in the process of experience sharing.

The distribution of the sensible is based on a set of mechanisms which oversee and control the field of possible experiences as well as the forms of their representation in social interaction. As a complex process of social reproduction it is formed in a field of social antagonisms and it attempts to regulate their outcomes in favor of the existing social organization. We should not understand the distribution of the sensible as an established condition of social homogeneity but rather as an evolving project of social normalization (in Michael Foucault's understanding of the term, 2009) that necessarily is open to contestation. In order for an imposed horizon of experiences and human relations to be accepted as natural a continuous support from representations of society (including representations of crucial sectors of social life as work, inhabiting, health etc.) is needed, which manages to convince society's members of its necessity, efficacy, morality, stability etc. In other words, dominant representations of society must naturalize and de-historicize existing social relations.

However, humans are not merely subjected to mechanisms of control which merely produce unavoidable patterns of behavior. Bourdieu insists that it is dispositions that are being inculcated through social training, generating schemes for possible action rather than direct instructions on how to behave and think. Dispositions, thus, mark and seek to define a field of possible actions rather than determine actions and subjects of actions unequivocally.

The fact that Bourdieu recognizes that "a struggle over representations in the sense of mental images" (1991: 221) is
unavoidable, actually stems from such a grounding of social
normalization on dispositions (rather than on fixed determina-
tions). Representations are, as are actions, the result of inculcated
dispositions activated in different life contingencies. No matter
how well structured social life aspires to be (or, actually, how
well structured dominant elites aspire to keep social life), differing circumstances (including historical crises or discontinuities in the life trajectories of certain individuals) may produce
incoherencies between dispositions or abrupt clashes between
normalized expectancies and social potentialities. A struggle over
representations may be latent, in a status of implicit disobedience, or become an explicit conflict which employs "new" and
"old" weapons. Indigenous world-views ("old" weapons) were
employed in such struggles in the context of anti-colonial culture
wars. Also, innovative representations of gender or work relations have been employed to shake established dispositions in
different societies ("new" weapons, as, for example, introducing
gender equality images in the patriarchal Kurdish culture in the
context of contemporary Kurdish liberation struggles).

Dominant as well as counter-dominant or dissident representations of society as a whole or of specific social relations need to
draw their means from social experience. Space as the matrix and
shaping factor of social experiences acquires a crucial role both
in the establishing of the distribution of the sensible and in the
challenging of its premises and its limits.

Thinking through space

Thinking and employing spatial relations in the expression of
shared thoughts and aspirations is a way of taking part in "struggles over representations." One can employ images of spaces to
express experiences and to illustrate thoughts. At this level, representations of spaces acquire the power to represent the kind of
social life that inhabits them, albeit selectively. Representations of
such a kind may become emblematic condensations of exemplary
practices contributing, thus, to the corroboration of existing dis-

positions. Moreover, dispositions themselves may be inculcated in early periods of formative education through spatial representations made available to the new members of a society as a means to shape their behavior and thinking.

A deeper, and thus more crucial, level of implication of spatial representations in social life is that which connects space-as-form with the production and not merely with the expression of thoughts. Maybe Walter Benjamin, more than any other thinker, has understood the importance of this way of thinking; he even made it a generative process in his writings and in the formation of his critical approach to modernity's emancipatory potential.

Benjamin both practices and philosophically explores thinking-in-images. As Sigrid Weigel formulates it, "thinking-in-images constitutes his specific and characteristic way of theorizing, of philosophizing and of writing" (1996: 53). And, thus, she proposes that "images are not the object, but rather the matrix and medium of his theoretical work" (1996: x).

Thinking-in-images means thinking through images. And this ability is not merely the accomplishment of an idiosyncratic thinker. It is more like a human capacity, developed in different ways and levels according to specific historic contingencies. Scientific reasoning is supposedly devoid of this kind of thinking that may be misleading or even mythologizing. Susan Sontag has shown (to name just one example), how, indeed, such a form of thinking nevertheless controlled both the description of AIDS and of cancer as diseases by medical discourse and how this deeply impacted on the dominant social meaning as well as on the research focused on the treatment of these diseases (1978, 1989). Images of war infest and guide both the understanding of the disease mechanism and its interception (confrontation being one more war image).

Thinking-in-images gives Benjamin the means to criticize modernity by thinking through the images of the modern city. As we know, he was not an urban theorist, and his interest in modernity's exemplary metropolises (mainly Berlin and Paris) was generated from his aim at unearthing modernity's potentialities. The modern city, according to him, was not merely reflecting representations of typical modern experiences but was, rather, shaped as a quasi-geological stratified formation bearing witness to the historic potentialities characteristic of modernity's discontinuous project. The city, thus, was not approached as a stock of images to be employed in order to illustrate a criticism of modernity. Spatial images, spaces-as-images, were considered as the means to think about modernity, as means to develop ways of thinking that ventured to find something new about modern life rather than demonstrate something already well known through images.

Maybe Benjamin, in his way, becomes deeply involved in a specific "struggle over representations" when he questions modern phantasmagoria as projected in the images of Paris "the capital of the nineteenth century" (1983). It is not that he only deconstructs modern phantasmagoria by revealing the ambiguities and distorted promises of the mythology of progress. He actually thinks through the images of urban phantasmagoria in search of "thought-images" which can further explore such a mythology in search of its hidden emancipatory potential. In the images of the great brand-new boulevards or the Parisian arcades Benjamin finds these potentialities (1999, especially Convolute L).

To promote thinking-in-images as a practice that interprets (and thus potentially challenges) firmly established dispositions is indeed a project of social criticism. However, this project is based on human capacities that may or may not be developed according to predominant norms of social behavior. Thinking-in-images may merely be the substratum of social consensus. And images of spaces have in many societies been used as a means to regulate and shape the thinking of those societies' members. For example, planning the city-as-image was in many cases a means to legitimize as natural (or God-given, or as part of a cosmological order) a certain social structure. Richard Sennett refers to such practices during the development of the Roman Empire as imposed policies which "had made order and imperial power inseparable" (1994: 89). "Visual order" was thus the way to establish a mode of thinking about society based on the predominance of a "reassuring geometry" (1994: 90).

The potentiality of space commoning

Concrete social realities have their spaces. They unfold in and through space. It is by interacting with spatial attributes and characteristics that the experience of individuals and groups unfolds. If every society reproduces itself by reproducing the habits and structural relations of its members, then the regulating of shared experiences is among the most powerful means to pursue this goal. Spatial arrangements, however, are more than containers of social life and shared experiences. Spatial arrangements interact with social experiences both by giving them concrete context and by supporting representations of those experiences which actually make them sharable. By being an active co-producer of social life and of the experiences which characterize it, space becomes a powerful means to control the distribution of the sensible. Let us remember Rancière's definition: "I call the distribution of the sensible the system of self-evident facts of sense perception that simultaneously discloses the existence of something in common and the delimitations that define the respective parts and positions within it" (2006: 12). This process actually channels sense perception to socially imposed patterns which are connected with meaningful representations of the social world. The perception of spatial forms and characteristics is part of this kind of social ordering. The normalization process, which lies at the foundations of social ordering, tries to ensure that future experiences will be according to deeply embedded "dispositions," a term Bourdieu uses to describe the results of socially inculcated tacit knowledge (1977, 2000).

However, what makes space a means to control both the shared experiences and their representations, gives space the power to shape *possible experiences*. A way of exploring this power is by thinking-in-images (Stavrides 2016: 209–227). In this case, the power to construct representations of social life through spatial qualities is used to project elements of possible social worlds through thought-images of possible spaces of social life. We know, of course, that the history of utopias is a history of utopian sites, utopian worlds, utopian cities, and utopian spaces, in many cases envisaged, depicted, or narrated in the greatest of detail. What distinguishes thinking-in-images from this history of utopian spatial projections is the fact that thought-images can be hybrid combinations of thoughts about a possible future and of spatial relations related to this future (conceived diagrammatically rather than in full imagistic detail). The term, which originated in the writing of the Frankfurt School theorists (Benjamin, Adorno, Bloch, and Kracauer), "self-consciously exposes the inescapable contamination of the theoretical by the figurative" (Richter 2007: 25). Thought-images, thus, do not offer (or seek to construct) depictions of a possible future but rather shape arguments about the future developed through the processing of images. Here lies the emancipatory potential of this process: a possible emancipatory future is both connected to the concreteness of available shared experiences and to their shared representations, as well as to that abstract generalizing reasoning which learns from such experiences and representations (and does not use them merely as examples or illustrations).

If emancipation has to do with the envisioning and testing of specific forms of social organization, possible spaces (understood as imagined arrangements or as specific possible sites) may become the means of both envisioning and testing those forms. Space, concrete and relational, abstract and specific, is truly connected to a crucial human capacity: to understand experience and imagine the world through arrangements of objects and subjects. Through space and spatial attributes (e.g. distance) humans make their experiences meaningful but they also long to reach beyond what they face as reality.

A comparison with the capacity of language may be instructive. This capacity is considered to be innate: humans may produce languages as part of their species-specific armature for survival (Virno 2009: 98–99). Language, thus, may take different forms in different historical periods, but also different levels of this capacity are being reached by different individuals in different language communities. In every case, however, language is an area of potentiality. To use Virno's suggestion, linguistic potentiality is never exhausted in the specific utterance or "speech act" which is actualized in different contingencies. Potential becomes the measure of what actually exists (in the case of language of what is uttered) but it is also the very precondition of going beyond it (2015a: 23–26).

What seems to be common to Virno and Giorgio Agamben is an effort to rescue human capacities from their direct exploitation by current capitalism, which they consider not merely as a distinct production system but also as a form of government based on biopolitics (Lemke 2011, Campbell and Sitze 2013, Wilmer and Žukauskaite 2016). Of course, they both focus on language as the most important human capacity which connects and even directs all the other capacities. And it is language, according to both of them, that is completely instrumentalized in contemporary work relations and production relations as a generic ability that all humans can employ. Actually, it is language, instrumentalized in the form of an all-pervasive communicability, which subordinates human communication to productive work (through information and telecommunication technologies) and to the shaping of consumption habits (especially through the mass media as well as the social media). Thus, according to Agamben, "in the society of the spectacle, it is this very communicativity [the communicative essence of human beings], this generic essence itself (that is language as *Gattungswesen*), that is being separated in an autonomous sphere. What prevents communication is communicability itself" (2000: 84).

To reclaim human capacities from direct capitalist exploitation, to restore communication as the ground of human community means, for Agamben, to restore the potentiality inherent to those capacities. Drawing heavily on Aristotle's problematization of potentiality (*dynamis*), Agamben suggests that potentiality is not and should not be exhausted to its actualizations. For the "coming community" (Agamben 1993) to be different from existing forms of social organization which are based on "belonging" and on identity categorizations and hierarchies, we need to restore potentiality as the basis of the common. "We need to secure a pure potentiality that does not pass over into actuality" (Brown 2013: 174). "We need to think man ... as a being of pure potentiality (*potenza*) that no identity and no work could exhaust" (Agamben 2014: 69).

Pure potentiality becomes the power of means, the power of

mediality, once it is released from its necessary connection to specific social ends, or, more specifically, once it is released from actuality as potentiality's necessary outcome. Politics becomes, for Agamben, "the sphere of pure means" (2000: 60), "the sphere of a pure mediality without end intended as the field of human action and of human thought" (2000: 117).

It is in such a prospect that potentiality will become the common denominator of shared life in a "coming community." Singularities will be shaped in "forms-of-life," in ways of living in which "mediality" (form considered as means without end) is to become the only distinguishing factor. "What is at stake then, is a life in which the single ways, acts and processes of living are never simply facts [therefore imprints for governance and rule making] but always and above all possibilities of life, always and above all potentiality (*potenza*)" (2014: 73).

The capacity to produce spaces and to think through spaces is indeed a human capacity which, as language, is never reducible to concrete social realities. This capacity corresponds to a potentiality that transcends any actual social reality. Virno believes that what he names as "potentials" "attest to human beings' poverty of instinct, undefined nature and characteristic constant disorientation" (2015a: 87). Stressing the importance of human disorientation as the condition of human life he insists: "Potential is intimately connected to disorientation" (2015a: 88), which results from the "lack of a pre-given *environment* in which we can take an innately secure place once and for all time" (2015a: 88, emphasis in original).

Using a different reasoning, Agamben comes to a conclusion that can be considered as similar. For him, man "appears as the living being that has no work, that is, the living being that has no specific nature and vocation" (Agamben 2007: 2). However, the capacity to think and act by employing spatial attributes and spatial denominators (such as, for example, distance, height etc.) cannot be rescued from its instrumentalization in capitalist society the way Agamben seems to suggest referring to language and life (life as form). Pure potentiality in terms of space will mean an absolute emphasis on the mediality of space completely cut off from any of its concretizations in lived human environments. Reduced to a means without end, space will be closer to the abstract space of capitalist production which is so severely condemned as alienating by Henri Lefebvre (1991: 50–53).

True, we can compare this abstract "spaceness" of space to the pure communicability that destroys communication, which Agamben connects with the conditions of capitalist exploitation of human capacities. There is, however, a crucial difference. Space as capacity is developed through experiences of actual spatial arrangements. The power to think beyond those actual arrangements and their material existence is developed from those experiences. Thus, we may retain the effort to keep open the potentialities related to this capacity only if we continuously open possibilities to experience different actual spaces. The actualization of spatial potentialities further opens the field of potentialization.

Spaces, concrete lived spaces, are works (the result of labor), but also the means to shape possible future worlds. Lefebvre's call for the right to the city to be established and defended is combined with an understanding of the possible emancipated urban society as a society which produces itself through collective creativity. This society will be "an *oeuvre* and not a product" (1991: 149). And this creativity is possible because "the urban remains in a state of dispersed and alienated actuality, as kernel and virtuality" (1991: 148). Virtuality is the crucial word: for Lefebvre, the city, as well as the urban society which inhabits it, is a "virtual object," a condition of human coexistence full or potentialities. Moreover, the real includes the possible, "the preconditions for another life have been created" (1991: 189). "Thus the city does not merely express the possible, it makes it factually possible, imaginable, because it reveals what is already there ready to be reclaimed" (Nadal-Melsió 2008: 170).

This is actually an approach to human emancipation that actively supports the creative capacities of people. We know that there are some harshly imposed limits to these capacities in present capitalist urban societies (2008: 170) However, not only explicit resistances to the inequalities of those urban worlds exist but also everyday collectively organized survival tactics, which produce potentialities of different forms of social organization.

In many parts of the world the poor, the excluded, the marginalized, those deprived of opportunities to develop "non-ordinary"
forms of life, actually re-invent the city as an area of sharing, and
sharing as a form of social coexistence. They actually combine
the potentialities which emerge in and through sharing with the
virtuality of the city. To return to Lefebvre once again, we need to
support through practice an "urgent utopia ... a style of thinking
turned towards the possible in all areas" (2009: 288)

Following Lefebvre's idea that the city is the collective "oeuvre"
of its habitants (1996: 173–174), we may conclude that the
potentialization of space is a result of commoning, the result
of sharing aspirations but also of working together, of working
in common. Lived spaces are shaped through human interactions which develop shared worlds. To potentialize those shared
worlds, which means to challenge their meaning and their power
to present the distribution of the sensible as an indisputable order
of life, people have to activate the potentialities of commoning.
And this essentially amounts to the liberation of commoning
from capitalist command.

Agamben thinks that in the feast "what is done – which in
itself is not unlike one does every day – becomes undone, is ren-
dered inoperative liberated and suspended from its 'economy'"
(2014: 69). Similarly, dance is the "liberation of the body from
its utilitarian movements" and the poem is rendering language
inoperative, "in deactivating its communicative and informative
function in order to open it to a new possible use" (2014: 70). In
all those cases, it seems, potentiality is really experienced as the
expansion of the field of the possible because there exist human
movements which are not dance and because there is a variety
of human discourses (human interactions through language)
which are not poetic. "Inoperativity" in this context defines a
describable externality, although the boundaries between the
poetic and the non-poetic (as well as those between dance and
everyday gestures) are socially marked. The potentialization of
everyday gestures, everyday language, or everyday acts of survival
does not happen, however, because we become able to render
them inoperative but, rather, because the externality of dance,
poetry and feast, respectively, is only relative historically: it is by

contaminating everyday normality that art or collective joy may transform it. Potentialization is a dynamic contingent process which transforms habits, and not the restoration of an unpolluted, ontologically different beyond.

Thus, to think about space as potentiality is to connect experiences of space to possibilities of expanding them and transcending them. To explore the potentialities of space is to explore the potentialities of spatial relations and the ways those relations may happen. Materiality is not merely an aspect of the actualization of spatial potentialities in a specific context but an essential constituent of the potentiality of space.

Space becomes potential when it is performed. And performance is not only a process of repetition, a process of normalization based on spatially acquired dispositions. Performing space, performing through space, is always open to discovering space through concrete performances, much like a dancer discovers possible movements by dancing and an actor possible gestures by acting or by rehearsing. By performing space we may transform actually existing spaces. Performing space actually means performing social relations, it means experiencing them as concrete unfolding realities, rather than as abstract definitions of social identities. And this is a way to live potentiality by creating it.

Maybe "what is at issue in Agamben's thinking of potentiality is simply and intensely creation – creation in its most radical form, a form that, to truly create, must make the complete of the dictated incomplete, must grasp decreation" (Deladurantaye 2000: 22). Creation, however, may become the substratum of a multiple process of displacements and experiments which unfold in myriad ways both in everyday practices and in moments of rupture. Creation is both mundane and heroic, as is the process of potentializing space. Rendering space inoperative is no way of discovering possible spaces. Destroying the instrumentalization of space imposed by capitalist governance may possibly become the motor of potentialization of space. But this is something that is necessarily exposed to the messy contradictions of lived reality.

Possible spaces

One can even go further in challenging the emancipating promise of pure potentiality: potentiality should never be reduced to the actual only because the actual always feeds potentiality. To go beyond what exists we need to use the experiences and thoughts that are born in what exists and struggle to transcend it.

Spatial capacity, the faculty to perceive through spatial attributes and to think through spatial attributes, can be said to be part of the ability of humans to create their own history, to be members of societies which unfold in history. This capacity shapes specific spaces but also may support the projection into future possible spaces of characteristics of experiences which unfold in the present. In Virno's theory the process through which potentials shape the present is not equated to actualization. For him, potential is pre-historical and non-chronological (2015a: 186–187). It "is the unrealized past against which the living measures itself while it lives" (2015a: 120). Potential, thus, cannot be connected to a certain moment in the past but it can be evoked by memory as that which measures the present. Potential always remains "unrealized" but, for this reason, we can say that it gives meaning and attributes value to actual experiences.

It is interesting to observe how Virno treats Benjamin's approach to the past. Benjamin's theory on history is based on the idea that historical time is full of discontinuities and ruptures, and therefore a narrative reconstruction of the past is only illusionary and mythologizing (Benjamin 1992a: 255). Moreover, such a narrative approach is essentially part of the mythology of continuous progress, which, transposed to politics, legitimizes a social-democratic view of social change as gradual and linear (1992a: 252). Ruptures indicate, for Benjamin, moments which reveal potentialities. Unrealized potentialities in the past can provide us with a knowledge which is crucial for the present: how to pursue a different future, an emancipatory future, by taking advantage of potentialities that were not followed in the past; by trying to win where others have lost (1992a: 247).

This approach to potentiality, to the potential, according to Virno, needs to be supplemented by an interpretation of the present's relation to potential. It is because the "present moment itself entails the past-in-general – potential – as one of its intrinsic components" (2015a: 144 note), that the present can be connected to a specific past and thus become meaningful in the prospect of social change. Potential makes the historical past a dynamic challenge for the future. Potential keeps the past as an unresolved pendency in the present.

There is something very useful here for a possible theory of the potentialities of space (or for space as part of the potential). If past and present experiences, shared (and thus socialized) through representations, actually provide people with the means to construct possible visions of a different future, then it is important to see the past not as a finished and fully describable reality but as a propelling force for the discovery of potentialities in the present. Re-activating the past might mean using, among other ways, images of the past, spatial configurations of past experiences, in order to discover in them potential spaces and potential spatialities. In the process of printing the images of the past with the powerful developing solutions of the present (an image that alludes to a technology of image printing made obsolete by contemporary xerography), spatial characteristics acquire new meanings, appear in new light, and are transformed or possibly distorted (but, of course, an initial "authentic" form of space is just as imaginary as any of its projections). To put it in other words, to see spaces of the past as opportunities to rethink what may change or what should change, necessarily entails the capacity to think through space, to construct possible spatialities.

Considering space, then, as a capacity to experience and to think of different forms of social organization, links space to the project of social emancipation. This does not amount to reiterating that new societies need new spaces. Emancipated societies, societies in which human emancipation unfolds, produce and need new spatialities, new ways, that is, to understand and employ space as a crucial factor of shaping human relations. Spatial potentialities support creative explorations of possible human relations.

Space and prefigurative politics

By focusing on space as potentiality, and by acknowledging
the capacity to think and act through space as a crucial human
capacity, we can reformulate the problem of prefiguration and
prefigurative politics. The simple and historically most enduring
way to conceive of prefigurative politics is as those practices in
which means reflect (mirror, look like) the ends. In prefigurative
politics, visions of a different society are supposed to shape struggles to establish such a society according to the same values that
support these visions (Breines 1982, Van de Sande 2017).There
is, of course, an important problem that makes the comparison
between means and ends highly precarious. We experience acts
as they unfold in time. And we can connect them to scopes either
judging by ourselves or by taking into account words or other
forms of expression which are used by the subjects of those acts
to explain what they aim at. There is, however, an unbridgeable
gap between words and deeds, scopes and acts, discourses and
practices. Actually, what we try to compare cannot really be
compared.

We can observe and judge acts (including the performance
status of enunciations) but scopes we have to infer. And words
that declare scopes merely do that: declare. Should we not then say
that acts reveal (according, of course, to an interpretative stance)
scopes rather than pre-figure them? Shouldn't we realize that acts
(including enunciating acts) may indeed be considered as a means
to accomplish something but ends can only be inferred? And,
surely, results of actions do not necessarily establish (let alone
"prove") the scopes of those actions. John Holloway suggests,
in his subtle definition of prefigurative struggles, an interesting
way out of this conceptual impasse. A "consciously prefigurative"
struggle "aims, in its form, not to reproduce the structures and
practices of that which is struggled against, but rather to create
the sort of social relations which are desired" (2002: 153–154).

By talking about the "form" of struggle, Holloway possibly tries
to show that means can be considered as forms rather than as
concrete realities, the way the realities of acts are. Focusing on the
formal aspect of acts may establish a common ground between

acts and scopes. What need to be compared are not acts and scopes but the forms of acts and scopes. Values in both acts and scopes can, therefore, be connected to their forms through which they are embedded in social relations. And what seems to differentiate those forms is power. It is because power relations take different forms that we can distinguish between different forms of relations between people. A certain society's members enter into differentiated social relations because of an overall arrangement of power distribution which characterizes this specific society.

Direct democracy and horizontality are forms of relations which construct modes of social organization based on the values of equality. Specific ways of distributing and controlling power are developed in the spatio-historical context of groups or societies which establish such relations. And, of course, those ways are being developed in time: forms characterize relations but in a way that is open to the historicity of struggles – forms are open to transformation. Prefiguration is actually being performed and prefigurative practices do not prefigure a future condition but actually prefigure a future process by unfolding as a process.

Commenting on the prefigurative politics of the alter-globalization movement, M. Maeckelbergh seems to suggest exactly this. Namely, that this movement was not creating "a prefiguration of an ideal society or type of community or abstract political ideology ... [but] ... a prefiguration of a process, a prefiguration of a horizontal decentralized democracy, which is at once a goal and current practice of the movement" (Maeckelbergh cited in Van de Sande 2013: 232).

Returning to space as capacity: spaces can be pre-figurative because they can show possible arrangements of social relations by way of analogy. Spaces do not simply illustrate or represent social relations that may inhabit them; they contribute in the shaping of those social relations. It is because space is both a medium (analogically able to show possible new ways of inhabiting) but also part of the projected future, that space can prefigure and materialize, at the same time, a different social condition.

This gives the shared capacity to use space the power to contribute to prefigurative politics by destroying the considered as indisputable polarity between means and ends. In actual spaces people can experience the future (the "end") and the means to reach it. Space, when it becomes enmeshed in prefigurative politics, is both experienced and potential, an actual materiality of arrangements and a dynamic construction of possible human relations which unfold in the present. Space as potential is more like a testing ground for the future: through real-time experiments parts of the future are brought to the present.

Space acquires its relational power, its power therefore to become a medium but also an aspect of social relations, through the shaping of its form: space-as-form is connected in three ways of social life. As the next chapter shows, space-as-form connects to social organization (form-as-organization), to the expression of social values and meaning (form-as-expression) and to the processes of labor and technology (form-as-materialization).

It is because space is shaped as form through social practices that space may be potentialized in prefigurative politics. Space is part of social life and not a way to establish a pure externality of life as it unfolds in a certain society. This is why space may be experienced and thought both as an external and an internal reality when it is part of prefigurative politics. Pre- does not exactly describe its status in terms of time: (pre)figurative spaces unfold on multiple levels of temporality – they may connect actual and remembered experiences with aspirations and dreams. And this multi-valence of practices may happen during the process in which space is actually produced in action.

An activist fighting for indigenous rights in Mexican Chiapas is actually juxtaposing different temporalities in spaces which are potentialized through collective actions of resistance: a remembered space of community, a sought-for space for indigenous autonomy, and an experienced space of everyday struggle are co-present in *territorio Zapatista* (Zapatista territory). Zapatista territory, thus, does not exist outside the capitalist Mexican state and the global flows which shape it. It emerges as an unfolding potentialization of dominant spatial relations in an effort to create expansive networks of commoning and self-governance. This is the meaning of Zapatista autonomy, which is clearly distinguished from the declared autonomy of whatever state.

As shown in most of the following chapters, emancipatory

commoning practices potentialize space through processes which overspill the boundaries of established places bearing established identities. Such practices open pores in the existing perimeters of contemporary enclave spaces and thus open established communities to potential newcomers, who can contribute to expanding circuits of sharing. A spatiality of passages supports this process of expansion. Threshold-like spaces may both support and express commoning as a dynamic process that travels through networks of collaboration and sharing that feed it. Enclosure, as it is very well described by historians of the commons (especially Peter Linebaugh), is the spatial practice of appropriating what used to be common, shared by all. Space commoning may thus construct spatial forms which express the emancipatory values of sharing by differentiating themselves both from the abstract forms of empty, homogeneous space and from the concrete forms of those saturated and identity-bound spaces that we call *places*.

We may approach territory as a kind of shared space which is necessarily connected to site-specific particularities of cultural meaning but, at the same time eludes a strict spatio-temporal definition. True, authorities and states tend to define "their" territory and to fight against adversaries and enemies in order to control, extend, and name it as "theirs." Territory, however, can be understood as encompassing the struggles to define it as well as the acts of extending its limits, both considered as processes that shape concrete ways of potentializing space. Places are static, territories are dynamic. Places are identified and identify, territories emerge as contested terrains of social meaning. Charting is one of the most prominent practices through which sovereign authorities attempt to control the meaning of territories, and as we know, charting can never be absolutely final. Even in the era of satellite mapping, the allegory of a paroxysmal all-encompassing cartography as a means to control a territory, which was developed by Jean Baudrillard, remains effectively convincing. An emperor, who ordered the most accurate map of "his" empire, had to face a most humiliating failure. His geographers tried to make a map so accurate that it aspired to become the complete replication of the empire with all its trees, rivers, villages etc. And as Baudrillard poetically suggests, "a few shreds [of the map are] still discernible in the deserts" (1983: 1).

Territories of emancipatory commoning are shaped by practices that tend to extend to ever new areas of sharing, that tend to discover new things for sharing and new ways to share and, thus, to promote processes of subjectivation through sharing. Territoriality can be used as the term to encompass this peculiar ensemble of social relations and culturally embedded meanings which characterize a group's distinctive awareness of being a group. And territoriality can actually express a process rather that an established condition of embeddedness, since it is meant to indicate qualities, modalities, that is, of historically specific socio-spatial relations.

Territorialities of emancipatory commoning characterize most of the examples used to corroborate the argument of this book. And following their expressive power will be one of the targets of their specific analysis: territorialities of commoning simultaneously organize and express commoning in and through space. In search for possible spaces and practices of emancipation, we need to potentialize existing spaces and to potentialize existing practices. In other words we need to develop an inventive re-appropriation of the power of commoning.

2

Commoning architectures

Contested common worlds and the role of architecture

The role of public space in molding city politics has been extensively theorized and studied. The shaping of citizenship and the establishment of citizen rights have been connected to struggles over and in public space, as well as to discourses that problematize public space as a constituent element of public life. It would be accurate to say that public space has formed the terrain for crises of citizenship more often than it has provided the stable background upon which historically specific forms of citizenship are expressed and enacted.

Public spaces have always been sites of social contention. According to Marcel Hénaff and Tracy Strong, "public space is always a contestation over the legitimacy of what can be brought and what can be excluded from the life one chooses and is required to have in common with others" (Hénaff and Strong 2001: 4). This perspective figures public space as a dynamic arrangement of public acts and disputes over what should be considered "common." The very meaning of "common" finds its expression in the constitutive practices of inhabiting, sustaining, or transforming public space; however, common worlds are by no means taken for granted by all. Indeed, public spaces often purported to be common worlds – explicitly represented in and signified by glorious public buildings, squares, or monuments – are challenged through acts of contestation and social struggle as well as by practices that create other kinds of emergent common worlds in, against, and beyond existing public spaces.

Urban common worlds are always under construction and thus open to various forms of contestation. Modern and contemporary cities appear to be concrete social worlds that shape and express shared universes of meaning and action. No matter how complex and multileveled the spatiotemporal order of such cities might be, such an order aspires to establish a common world that contains recognizable social relations and patterns of social practice. Contemporary enclave cities develop as agglomerations of self-contained urban worlds in which corresponding citizen profiles and urban behaviors are being imposed. Many people have to inhabit neighborhood enclaves (gated communities or slums), many have to do their shopping in shopping enclaves (malls and large department stores); more extreme examples are corporate buildings, which are often fortress-like controlled areas, and public spaces under severe surveillance, which often end up being restricted areas for those who do not conform to specific behavior patterns. One thinks of sports enclaves (including Olympic facilities), which tend to evolve into exemplary spaces of so-called "crowd management." Ceremonial public spaces, however, are meant to indicate that an overarching common world can be identified with a specific society and condensed within its state institutions. This world is supposed to be emphatically connected with promises of social cohesion and peace. In urban public space, contemporary forms of domination thus appear as legitimate, productive, and suitable for the reproduction of the corresponding social order.

By this logic, public space becomes a site of contestation over the very possibility of the common. Jacques Rancière writes, for example, that politics "conceives community ... as a polemic over the common" (2010: 100). In other words, any social contestation that targets the meaning and reproduction of what is considered to be common within a specific society is, essentially, a political act. What reproduces existing arrangements of roles and practices does not deserve to be included as politics, according to Rancière. It is merely the expression of a society that perpetuates itself – a social arrangement that Rancière designates as a "police" order

(2010: 100.) It is questionable, however, to suggest that it might be possible for a society to remain totally stable and beyond internal antagonisms – and so outside the challenges of politics. Politics is present as long as there are disputes over the meaning, the value, and the form of the common – no matter how latent, implicit, or even distorted and disguised as obedience those disputes may be.

In point of fact, it seems that we live in a period in which politics, in the form of a polemic over the common, directly upsets the order of contemporary urban common worlds. And this is happening not only in the area of discourse or ideology but in the arena of practice as well. Different segments of the urban populations seem increasingly to distrust the very central shaping force of constructed common worlds: the state mechanisms along with the forms of social life imposed by state-regulated social relations. Displaced, marginalized, or disempowered populations in world metropolises reclaim their right to the city through struggles that emphatically redefine the area of the common (Wacquant 2008, Sassen 2014). In struggles to obtain or update urban transportation, in fights against the privatization of important urban resources and services, and in campaigns in support of decent housing and health and education facilities, people explicitly challenge the neoliberal architectonics of dominant common worlds. What James Holston has termed "insurgent citizenship" (2008) refers to this set of acts and demands, which targets inequalities that are evident in the everydayness of exclusion and discrimination. Insurgent citizenship challenges dominant ideologies that connect public space with forms of regulation which result in corroborating social inequalities. Moreover, Holston suggests that insurgent citizenship is connected to a "politicization of the oikos" (2008: 312). This means that the very limits that shape the domestic realm (oikos) are being questioned as people from the *periferias* of the metropolis construct their own community spaces (Lazar 2008, Zibechi 2007 and 2010).

It is not only that new kinds of urban space emerge but also new spatialities: new qualitative characteristics of space are being invented or re-defined, through which new social relations are being developed. In the process of challenging established common worlds, space (the site of experience and the means to represent it and to reflect upon it) is being activated as a source of social potentialities. Insurgent public spaces, politicized cohabitation practices, territorialities of resistance and new spatial arrangements aimed at promoting democratic forms of participation: all these are rich sources for spatial potentialities that shape social potentialities.

True, common space (as distinct from public space) existed and still exists in peri-urban and especially rural communities as a form of community-managed, shared space. It is beyond doubt that shared memories of displaced rural populations have contributed to the rediscovery of common space by peoples in their struggles to live in large and hostile cities. However, common space in urban contexts emerges today either in the form of public space appropriated by those who are excluded from it or in the form of collectively managed spaces meant to support a common urban life that creates new (and not simply traditional) social relations and bonds (Stavrides 2014: 546–550). For example, the precariat, marginalized, and peripheral populations house themselves in collectively reclaimed urban areas, often through practices of mutual help connected to shared worldviews that consider community as the center of human existence. One might cite, for instance, *mutirão* in Brazil (more about this in chapter 6), or *minga* in Andean countries (Colloredo-Mansfield 2009, Faas 2017), or *ubuntu* in South Africa (Swanson 2007, Letseka 2014). Latin American marginalized urban populations have in fact inventively rediscovered the uses and values of public space by reconstructing collective ways of producing and maintaining it. Landless worker movements and homeless movements not only struggle for life in urban and rural spaces but also often construct new relations between public and domestic space by focusing insistently on the importance of shared community spaces. A new kind of space seems to emerge in those urban collective experiences: common space.

Common space is not simply the space that corresponds to a distinct community and is used by those who belong to it. Although this is often the case – as, for instance, disempowered communities trying to defend a minimum common life by barricading themselves in shared enclaves — nevertheless, common spaces sometimes transcend the limits of the specific community that generated them. Common spaces remain open to newcomers, especially when the collective effort that produced them has not resulted in a stable community of users. This happened in recent urban struggles that were performed in and through public space occupations and that managed to create their own ephemeral but innovative and liberating forms of publicness. In the tent cities of the Arab Spring manifestations, in the Occupy and the Indignados-type square occupations (in London, Athens, Madrid, and other cities), in the Gezi Park (Istanbul), and Hong Kong self-managed temporary settlements of protest, as in so many other cases of urban mobilizations, people have created common spaces that were shaped through ongoing negotiations between diverse collective actors sharing a respect for differences and a longing for equality.

Distrust for the state, explicit clashes with unjust rules and forms of urban governance, and overt confrontations with exclusionary power arrangements may characterize the emergence of common space in today's metropolises. What is new, however, in the multiform and dispersed, but often networked and inventive, production of common spaces is "an always alert and always generous disposition towards the common" (Zibechi 2010: 136). Common space is a project and an exigency that emerges in contemporary urban conflicts as well as in dispersed collective survival initiatives. The contemporary metropolis is traversed by networks of cooperation and communication that produce not only tangible goods but also forms of sharing, knowledges, affects, habits, and forms of collective action (Hardt and Negri 2009, Roggero 2010). Common-space experiences emerge in different practices of everyday collaboration, which either escape capitalist control and command or unfold in a tense relation with market and state mechanisms. Common space is both a potential means of developing commoning practices and the stakes or scope of such practices. This is why it seems crucial for any attempt to go beyond contemporary forms of domination to be able to learn from the diverse practices that make common space happen, to experiment with common space production, to explore common space spatialities as spatialities distinct from dominant "enclavism" (Atkinson and Blandy 2005 and 2017), and to reclaim existing public spaces as common spaces. Collective experiences, shared knowledges and common aspirations (often expressed in shared thought-images) intersect in such multifarious projects. Common space and practices of commoning-through-space emerge as forms of potentialization of space which hint towards possible emancipatory futures.

This chapter will explore the role architecture may assume in developing an awareness of the potentialities of space and in searching for spatialities of emancipation. If it is to connect with social experiments of human emancipation in the context of today's capitalist enclave city, architecture needs to potentialize itself. Architecture needs to become part of urban worlds in movement, shared urban worlds, that is, in which the dominant distribution of the sensible is challenged and shaken.

Architecture can be considered an intellectual practice that focuses on the shaping of space. Throughout its history as a profession or as a set of socially recognizable practices, architecture has produced ideas, projects, and buildings that were meant to provide space to be inhabited by different societies with differing values, priorities, and forms of production and reproduction. It seems, however, that architecture has not only been responsible for covering the demands of various authorities and satisfying the needs of the ruling classes but also of devising forms that would shape those needs and demands as well as those that might describe future or utopian societies. This is because, at least since the Renaissance, architecture has been an intellectual and not a simply a professional practice: it has been actively engaged in debates about social values and social meanings, taking part in what Pierre Bourdieu has described as "struggle[s] over representations" (Bourdieu 1991: 221). Thus, architecture has been part of politics in Rancière's sense of the word: it has contributed to various polemics over the common.

However, it is important to keep in mind that architecture is not merely a distinct form of discourse, although debates about space are often conducted in the arenas of architectural theory and architectural presentations. Architecture engages the polemics over the common as a practice of shaping space, as a practice that problematizes and explores spatial form. And here we must at least sketch the potentialities inherent in this practice that may indeed support struggles over the definition of the common, and especially the definition and uses of common space. Form, in fact, is the end product as well as the initial focus of architectural practice on at least three levels, each of which seems to influence the other.

1. Spatial form as organization: form can be considered as the overall arrangement of a specific set of spaces. From this perspective, a spatial construction or arrangement is the result of a specific set of organized, formalized spatial relations.
2. Spatial form as expression: form can be considered as the structuring of meaningful comparisons between spatial elements that are being articulated to express a coherent and recognizable statement of social meaning (such as a collective identity, a valuable lesson from the past, or the legitimization of an institution).
3. Spatial form as materialization: form can be considered as the result of certain acts that employ materials and technologies as well as social relations of collaboration in order to produce concrete arrangements of space (e.g., by concretizing those arrangements through specific material boundaries).

During the first "heroic" years of the Modern Architecture movement, for example, the complex problem of housing – considered as a social good to be made available to all members of industrial societies – was stated not simply as a new social need but, essentially, as a problem of form, as a problem of architecture. And it was confronted as a problem of organization (discussions on standards, on *Existenzminimum*, on types of mass dwelling, etc.), as a problem of expression (mass production expressing efficiency and equality, forms borrowed from machine aesthetics etc.), and as a problem of materialization (cooperation between various arts à la Bauhaus, modernist appeals for the industrialization of building construction understood as a set of technology and work relations, etc.). In other words, by exploring spatial form in each of these three levels, one can see that architecture may, at times, either

effectively reproduce dominant social values (and historically specific social needs) or gesture towards possible urban worlds.

Spatial form as organization

Common space, as we have seen, emerges today through practices linked to the everyday survival of the poor and the excluded,
as well as through practices of overt contestation that challenge
existing oligarchies and forms of political domination. In both
cases (as well as in cases in which both sets of practices converge),
common space cannot be described as a stable set of spatial
relations but rather as a set of spatial relations that are being
performed through practices of "urban commoning" – as in the
politicized homeless movements that seek to build new social
relations in their occupied buildings. If it is to remain different
from public and private space, common space must be a process.
This means that communities and collectivities need to plan those
spaces but also to make them happen: to create them by shaping
uses and rules of use in the process of inhabiting them.

   A crucial lesson to be learned from the practices of creating common space is that understood in terms of form-as-
organization, this space is not characterized by an arrangement of
parts that constitute a clearly demarcated area. Rather, this space
has an inherently relational character. Common space is more
like a threshold area, or a network of threshold areas that medi-
ates between spaces of diverse levels of privacy. What may look
like a miniature square, for instance, might be the common courtyard of a self-managed MTST settlement in Brazil (Movimento
dos Trabalhadores Sem Teto (Homeless Workers Movement, a
shack-dwellers' movement) – something more like a space with
porous and movable boundaries that are being shaped and transformed by those who collectively use it. Likewise, in the occupied
Syntagma square in Athens during the period of the worldwide
Occupy movement actions, space was constructed so that it was
no longer bounded by arrangements meant to regulate the uses
and meaning of a ceremonial no-man's land: Syntagma square
was converted to an expanding network of threshold spaces
hosting diverse micro-communities of commoning.

Can architecture study the characteristics of such spaces and propose forms of spatial arrangement that may contribute to their proliferation, making them at the same time more adjustable to the needs of urban commoners? We already have examples of such attempts. In the case of El Campo de Cebada in Madrid, for example, an empty sunken plot adjacent to an indoor market in La Latina neighborhood has been converted by active citizens to a very lively common space. After the demolition of a large municipal swimming pool in 2009, and because the economic crisis cancelled the municipality's development-through-privatization plans, a peculiar hollowed-out urban space has been transformed through citizen participation to a neighborhood common-space area, bounded by high walls. Intervention in that existing open space on a level that was lower than that of the surrounding streets produced innovative forms of theater-like spatial organization.

Porosity and multi-use urban furniture became the means to create spatial relations encouraging the participation of people in shifting boundaries between different segments of the area. Most

2.1 El Campo de Cebada in Madrid

2.2 El Campo de Cebada in Madrid: collectively created urban furniture for a shared common space

of the urban furniture was designed in experimental workshops focused on innovative recycling. Creators of smaller common spaces for groups of citizens focused on different initiatives and converted large parts of the available space to event stages without ceremonial overtones.

Another example is the Navarinou occupied park in Athens. In a collective neighborhood initiative that occupied a parking lot and converted it to a self-managed urban micro-park, participating architects worked together with all those residents involved in the initiative in order to collectively plan the area as a porous meeting place. This is multifarious common space that was produced by people determined to actively create an open space for public use at Exarchia (a neighborhood which was connected to many active movements and which had been one of the most important centers of December 2008 youth uprisings). It still evolves through innovative re-arrangements: new spatial elements are being devised that act as social micro-condensers.

For instance, a recently installed multi-use unit made out of a reshaped container box was designed by students of National Technical University of Athens, School of Architecture.

Spatial form as expression

In terms of form-as-expression, architecture can also contribute to the creation of common spaces. As an intellectual practice that may enter into battles over representations, architecture can experiment with possible forms of space that may represent types of communal life yet to be explored. True, architectural form cannot by itself ensure the potential communal, anti-authoritarian, and equalitarian uses of public space. Foucault was right in observing that there are no actual spaces of freedom but only practices of freedom: "I think that it can never be inherent in the structure of things to guarantee the exercise of freedom. The guarantee of freedom is freedom" (Foucault 2000: 355). And it is when "the liberating intentions of the architect coincide with the real practice of people in the exercise of their freedom" that architecture can produce positive effects in this direction (2000: 355). Architecture may catalyze collective practices oriented towards collective self-management (which seems to be the only socially meaningful performance of freedom) and even represent or prefigure emancipating social relations in arrangements of space meant to support them.

During the period between the two World Wars, architectural proposals to build new and more just social spaces (and hence a new and more just society) grew on the fertile ground of important social experiments in Europe. "Red Vienna," the Weimar Republic's *Grossiedlungen,* and Soviet Russia's early urban experiments in the collectivization of city life constitute an amazing heritage of utopian as well as innovatively realist projects in which the meaning and the values attributed to public space were extensively rethought (Miller Lane 1985, Tafuri 1990, Blau 1999). This was not the time yet, especially in the western world, for experimentations with common space, although the aim of designing a "new city" for the "new man" was connected to devising new communal spaces. Common laundry areas as

2.3 Karl Marx Hof social housing complex in Vienna: gesturing towards a liberated workers culture

well as kindergarten buildings in most of the new neighborhoods in Vienna, Frankfurt, and Berlin were more like extensions of the welfare state than genuine common spaces in which communities expressed their distinct values of cohabitation and themselves shaped the rules of commoning.

Architectural efforts to rethink spatial form as a means to express commoning values can, however, learn a lot from those important modernist socio-urban interventions between the wars. Specific questions arise from studying these early movements. Is it necessary, for example, to devise explicit architectural symbols that condense (in order to express) the values of common space? In Red Vienna, architects employed colossal statues to indicate the values of an emerging sought-for proletarian community destined to create a liberating future. Today's common-space architectural prefigurations may employ more modest means: a multiplicity of architectural symbols evoking different cultures and encouraging cross-fertilizations; recognizable everyday forms of common life

2.4 Expressing a new Protean (or Faustian?) ethos (a housing complex of "Red Vienna")

recuperated from their extensive appropriation by consumerism; emblemizings of environmentally aware cultures and markers of energy-saving and recycling ethics, and so on.

In contrast to most modernist holistic and programmatic architectural gestures that tried to devise utopian forms to express a preconceived future, today's architecture may need to express commoning as a set of practices oriented towards difference rather than sameness. The legendary Byker Wall, regarded as one of the UK's best postwar council estates, is an example of such an effort to express shared community values through architectural form by differentiating, at the same time, the facades and layout of different apartment types. Although this was the result of a participatory design process, and the leading architect, Ralph Erskine, was explicitly inspired by Swedish social-democratic welfare ideas, Byker Wall did not escape the fate of social housing complexes that eventually became areas of solitude and alienation (Minton 2015). On the other hand, in contrast, New Urbanism's proposals are connected to a re-invention of the diverse urban housing typologies in traditional US cities, in the context of planning new neighborhoods or cities (as, for example, Celebration City in Florida). They thus have only superficially contributed to expressing values connected to designed shared spaces. Architectural form, in this latter case, becomes the means to create scenery for simulated space-commoning. Common space needs to reflect the power of active comparisons with previous and existing projects and embrace everyday negotiations between communities of difference if it is to sustain encounters that aim at producing inclusive common worlds.

Spatial form as materialization

Shaping possible common spaces through processes of materialization in suggested or discovered spatial forms is also an important aspect of architecture's contribution to space commoning. Materialization does not refer only to the actual processes of construction; it also necessarily includes forms of work organization and relevant acts of knowledge sharing. Participative planning and "cooperative design" are practices that generate proposals through the active participation of potential users in the planning of the proposed design. The long history of such architectural and urban planning experiments, which dates back to the "advocacy planning" practices of the 1970s, includes cases in which the future users of urban space were also directly involved in proposal development and implementation.

Spatial form has always been a contested social terrain. Administrative decisions and implemented urban policies are the result of choices connected to political and social priorities as well as to power arrangements expressing specific interests. So, who decide in which way specific urban problems will be solved, implicitly or explicitly, shapes the form of city space. Ranging from master-plans to plans for small neighborhood urban facilities, such decisions prescribe future uses of space and express specific values in spatial form. What makes a lot of difference is the way such decisions are actually implemented in specific areas of the city and the ways they are challenged (through words as well as in action) by those who oppose the choices made.

Depending on the ways potential uses of space are included in deliberations or decision-making processes concerning the way space is planned, spatial form is given a concrete material existence which reflects the processes that made its existence possible. Concerning the participation of those affected by the planning choices, in the formulation of these choices, and in debates that explained the field of potential solutions to problems of urban spatial form, a long history of different practices can be traced.

Advocacy planning was introduced as a term by the planner Paul Davidoff in 1965. As he states, "advocacy becomes the means of professional support for competing claims about how the community should develop" (1965: 48). In his support for plural planning he considers public interest as a contested area explicitly connected with value-based prioritizations. And those who have less power and means to question the prioritizations which perpetuate urban and social injustices need to be supported by advocate planners (1965: 51).

Advocacy planning was, from its beginning, connected to the prospect of a just city and inspired many activist-planners to work in support of neighborhood associations and organizations of the urban poor, including the Black Power movement (Progressive Architecture 1968: 102). Shaping community spaces, resisting urban renewal plans which were to destroy the common life and shared resources of poor urban communities, and advocating against exclusionary land use decisions were among the tasks of advocate planners, which connected them to processers of space commoning (although the term did not exist back then).

Participation of future inhabitants in the planning and design of housing areas was especially promoted by architects who questioned the validity of universal spatial language promoted by heroic architectural modernism. Beginning with attempts connected with the Team 10 architects, who nevertheless haven't completely lost their faith in the universalist aspirations of modernism, important experiments showed that spatial forms may be developed through processes of participation on most levels of the production of space. Hasan Fathy's experiment for the design of the New Gourna settlement in Egypt shortly after the Second World War is highly indicative of this approach.

Fathy, an enlightened and visionary Egyptian architect, believed that he could produce a model village by directly involving the future inhabitants and by carefully observing the forms through which their society and culture was organized. Putting a great emphasis on the direct participation of the Gournii in the construction works of the settlement, he sought to revive, and to regain respect for, the traditional building craftsmanship (Fathy 1973: 40–43). Villagers were to be educated by able traditional craftsmen in order to be able to work in the building of houses and public spaces designed according to traditional forms of Arab architecture. Fathy's choices concerning spatial prototypes and architectural typologies are truly debatable (see e.g. Steele 1988). However, the constructed parts of the new village clearly reflect the process of design, the forms of participation of future inhabitants and the close relation of spatial form-as-materialization with the envisaged practices of community sharing in the model village.

Although Fathy's experiment was a failure in terms of the people's willingness to actually inhabit the new village (probably due to resistances developed against Cairo's bureaucracy and perhaps also due to distrust against modernizing experiments), it certainly proves that the process of developing spatial forms for cohabitation through collaboration creates shared experiences of potentially shared spaces. Fathy's envisioned collaborating trinity, owner, architect, and craftsman (Fathy 1973: 39), described a process of shared space production meant to shape practices of commoning within the context of a certain traditional society.

As chapter 5, devoted to the *Bon Pastor* project shows, advocacy planning can still be a source of space commoning experimentations and direct popular resistance against "urban renewal" plans. The chapter considers questions arising from the interconnected levels of action that shape spaces by directly affecting choices related to appropriate forms through popular participation and expert consultation.

Chapter 6, focusing on the USINA-centered participatory architectural design (Centro de Trabalhos para o Ambiente Habitado (Work Center of the Inhabited Environment)) will further extend the problematization of spatial form-as-materialization, exploring the ways construction methods employed and forms of homeless

2.5 Participatory planning in contemporary Brazil (a USINA work also commented upon in chapter 6)

movement members participation in the relevant discussions on the form of their future housing complexes are truly connected. USINA seems to suggest in practice that concrete materializations of spatial form may enhance commoning both by the discovery of housing typologies suitable to house a politicized community of commoners and in the actual collaboration developed during construction.

Architecture and the exigency of the commons

There are two crucial transverse questions regarding the three levels of architectural form discussed above. First, who is shaping the specific demand for space to which each specific architectural proposal answers? And furthermore, who is going to own the space to be produced and thus have the right to shape the rules of the space's use? Common space may indeed emerge against the directives of a certain authority that has planned it either as public space under certain conditions or even as private space (or public space to be offered to private profit making). Any kind of appropriation of public space that overspills the rules imposed by the authority responsible for its production will inevitably lead to contestation. And this, essentially, crosses all three levels of the architectural generation of form. All three levels can and do express differing forms of social antagonism and differing forms of polemic over the common. Urban issues at stake become arenas of urban conflicts. And urban conflicts result in different views and practices concerning the shaping of inhabited space. Architectural form is neither a definite solution to a problem posed by society nor efficient or successful regardless of the process through which it was articulated and the presuppositions on which it was based. Spatial form as organization is clearly connected to presuppositions regarding forms of common life, forms of coexistence, forms of definition of a common world. Spatial form as expression obviously touches upon issues of social values to be shared or to be denied. And spatial form as materialization directly raises questions that compare means and ends: is the resulting common space the product of commoning practices?

In addition, if the production of common space is to be considered a process that overspills the existing definitions of public space and confronts the authorities that tend to limit the dynamism of such space, then this process has to be evaluated according to the historically specific conditions of its emergence. Were those conditions favorable for practices that could possibly bypass state control or state paternalism? Could architectural form and commoning acts challenge existing embedded authorities? Could the production of common space avoid the suffocating embrace of market mechanisms?

There are in fact many cases of architectural experimentation in the shaping of common space that accept the economic or institutional support of state mechanisms. For example, the project of the Academy for a New Gropiusstadt works to convert mass housing settlements to "a model for a resilient urban environment" (Stollmann 2014: 134–135). Explicitly targeted to contribute to the "debate on commons and public welfare," this project encourages collaboration with residents as well as efforts to influence the decisions of institutional actors. One cannot simply dismiss such efforts as acts aimed at restoring trust in the state and to the welfare imaginary in periods of harsh neoliberalism. Struggles for and through common space are always historically specific. But if we want to try to imagine and support attempts at commoning that go beyond existing capitalism and domination, we will need to explore practices of common space production that directly oppose state and market interventions. USINA's work – based on a strong homeless movement – managed to shape the movement's demands on the local state of São Paulo and thus ensure that the final result was to be connected with collectively self-managed practices of space-commoning.

In a different way but with a similar spirit, occupied squares directly defied the market and the state in constructing their ephemeral common spaces inside emblematic public spaces of capitalist metropolises. These collective experiences of place-making were thus added to differing attempts to shape the polemic over the common by supporting popular participation in the definition of more inclusive and more just common urban worlds. In, against, and beyond capitalist enclosures, common space can trigger practices that gesture towards an emancipated society.

Architecture, as an intellectual practice that chooses to take sides in this process, may indeed contribute today to social experiments that will create glimpses of a liberating future. Equally distanced from both the fantasies of the avant-garde architect as the chosen creator of the future and the cynicism of the star architect in service of the state and the capital, today's engaged architects may modestly participate in collective efforts to imagine, visualize, produce, and use emerging common spaces. In those spaces, the seeds of tomorrow's emancipation are being carefully planted.

3

Territorialities of emancipation

Zapatista territory and Zapatista territoriality

Maybe Benjamin was right when he said that "More quickly than Moscow itself, one gets to know Berlin through Moscow" (Benjamin 1985a: 177). Let us not forget that Berlin was his home city whereas Moscow was a city he visited as a foreigner. What this chapter attempts to develop is a strategy similar to Benjamin's but this time with the explicit aim to explore a different kind of knowledge connected to spatial experience. What if, in order to understand what role space played in shaping alternative experiences of democracy and autonomy in the occupied squares of our cities (especially during the Occupy movement period), we focus on the experience and practices of Zapatista politics in faraway Mexican Chiapas? What if, through studying the building of autonomy in Chiapas, we can better understand insurgent assemblies in Athens, London, New York, Hong Kong, Istanbul, Paris, Tunis, Cairo, Rio …?

Space matters: space does not simply reflect or sustain existing relations between people. Space gives form to these relations. Especially in periods of crisis, new spatial arrangements seem to emerge along new relations and new forms of social organization. Maybe then we need to use different terms to approach the inherent spatiality of processes of social change. And critical geographers seem already to be aware of this need. Their discussion, focused on the meaning of territory and territoriality, is crucially important for the development of this book's argument on the power commoning has to potentialize lived space.

To understand the spatiality of commoning practices in the Zapatista self-managed communities, first we need to explore the very basis of Zapatista autonomy: Zapatista territory. In rural Chiapas one encounters some strange signs indicating areas described as Zapatista territory. However, no explicit boundaries may be observed which – we take this for granted – are necessary for a territory to be defined.

Thinking in terms of space, we cannot actually locate a strict inside and a strict outside of the Zapatista area. Village communities are scattered in the region of almost 74,000 km2: some of them are pro-Zapatista; some are mixed (including non-Zapatistas who, in many cases, however, use the facilities of the autonomous municipalities and often prefer the autonomous system of justice and health instead of the federal one); and some are controlled by the *"partidistas"* (those who support one of the institutional parties of Mexico). Besides, federal roads and highways cross the area, and federal electricity and telephone networks extend throughout most of the inhabited land. Notably, too, large military camps are situated near the most important Zapatista communities.

So, Zapatista territory, considered merely as space is not easily definable. One can even say that it only exists in a precarious state of hybridity. It is space both included in the Mexican state territory and, at the same time, excluded from it. Considering this socio-political experiment of autonomy in terms of space one is puzzled: Where is this autonomous area which, as we tend to suppose, should be clearly separated from the state-ruled one?

Andrea Brighenti suggests that we should reconsider the term territory by first agreeing that "territory is not an object and should not be confused with the space where it takes place" (2010: 56). "Territory is not defined by space, rather it defines spaces through patterns of relations. Every type of social tie can be imagined and constructed as territorial" (2010: 57). For Brighenti this approach is the necessary starting point for a potential scientific endeavor he calls "territorrology."

Carlos Walter Porto-Gonçalves and Enrique Leff seem to offer

3.1 Zapatista territory

a different perspective to a possible rethinking of territory as not merely space. Their point of view, which they situate in the emerging field of political ecology, was formed through engaged fieldwork oriented towards the study of localized environmental struggles, especially in Latin America.

They suggest that such struggles are predominantly connected to the "reinvention of territories" (2015). And a defining characteristic of such practices, according to them, is "the claiming of rights to their territory [by indigenous peoples] (2015: 73). What they describe as a "shift from the struggle for land to the claim for territory" (2015: 72) is an emerging set of struggles and collective acts which establish *new social relations and forms of social organization*. Claiming territorial rights is more than claiming their right to live where their ancestors used to live. It is claiming their right to live according to values and habits they share, and according to forms of organization they have created in order to reproduce their communities.

True, such territorial struggles may seem to be merely struggles

for a specific community's mode of existence. What, however,
connects those struggles with the problematics of commoning
(and especially with the prospect of emancipating commoning)
is the fact that those communities actually have coexisted and
co-evolved with important ecosystems (2015: 71) acquiring and
developing crucial knowledges focused on an "alternative social
rationality" (2015: 86), which amounts also to "an alternative
environmental rationality" (2015: 85). Territorial struggles of
those communities, thus, represent a kind of confrontation with
the state and market imposed capitalist social relations. In this
confrontation, territory is both a shaping factor and an issue at
stake.

   The nation-state constructs its territory as a set of rules, practices, and patterns of social relations, which amounts to a form
of governing a certain population living in a certain area, usually
clearly defined. As Stuart Elden suggests, commenting upon
Foucault's lectures on *Security, Territory, Population*, states, in
the era of security, exert their power through a "politics of calculation," which is manifested not only in the control of populations
but also in the control of territories. Thus, "Territory is more
than merely land, but a rendering of the emergent concept of
'space' as a political category: owned, distributed, mapped, cal-
culated, bordered and controlled" (Elden, 2007: 578). Territory
construction, however, is a process rather than an originary act of
a state. State territory is being reconstructed in and through social
antagonism, especially when dominant modes of life and production are being challenged. This is how "a number of projects of
territorialization can exist in the same physical location" (Reyes
and Kaufman 2011: 519).

   For Saskia Sassen, a prominent theorist on globalization, "the
relationship between territory and state authority today can
accommodate the existence inside national territory of denation-
alized spatialities" (2006: 418). This is a view from above that tries
to study the complexities of globalization processes by focusing
on assemblages of "territory authority and rights." A study from
below might see new emerging practices of territorialization
which express forces of resistance to contemporary globalized
capitalism. Zibechi's work emblematizes and concretizes this

approach by focusing on contemporary social movements in Latin America. His suggestion is that those movements and their struggles are territorialized, by especially seeking to secure spaces beyond state control and often in conflict with the market (2012: 14). Such "territories in resistance" are more like emerging areas of survival and struggle, especially for the urban poor, but essentially differ from the homogeneous (or homogenizing) enclaves of the traditional working classes in industrial capitalism. In those territories, the excluded (in terms of work opportunities, civil rights, race and gender equality, and cultural dignity) organize their resistances and their survival tactics by accepting diversity, and by profiting collectively from differences which are condemned, otherwise, to the same discriminating fate. Theirs is a struggle to increase difference rather than establish homogeneity.

This becomes a central issue in the discourse of Zapatistas when they refer to their *territorio*, as well as in the discourse of homeless activists involved in the construction of the autonomous neighborhoods of Mexico City. According to Zibechi, "political action on the margins," as he terms it, is characterized by "the politicization of social and cultural differences" (2012: 76).

This re-territorialization from below, which challenges the dominant territorial assemblages of globalization within the context of specific nation-states, seems to gesture towards a redefinition of territory: "territories in resistance" are expanding and inclusive spaces-in-the-making, which house, protect, and express specific collectivities of struggle but they also mitigate, interconnect and open themselves to potential networks of urban solidarity and cooperation.

Territories in resistance are porous territories. This does not mean that they are unbounded or undefined by those who inhabit and produce them. Porosity describes their inherent potentiality to keep on interacting with their surrounding areas in a process of transmitting resistance practices. Movement activists often stress the importance of the protection of resistances which they connect with defense arrangements. And the prioritization of defense arrangements almost automatically leads to images of enclosed spaces. However, the power of resistance, as well as the prefigurative potential of commoning practices that characterize resistance territories, unfold when boundaries (even defensive ones) are being transcended. Territories in resistance need to be threshold-like spaces, passages in the making rather than barricaded enclaves of otherness. Of course, in certain historical moments, even barricading may become necessary in order to secure the future metastatic effect of the resistance virus. But this needs to be a temporary strategy. The best protection of resistance territories is their proliferation.

Porto-Gonçalves and Leff deduce that "National State [is] a territory inhabited by multiple territorialities" (2015: 72). Social antagonism and alternative forms of life coexist in the state territory and it is due to specific circumstances that this coexistence may become explosive or even acquire transformative power. Communities which produce "alternative social rationalities," then, actually support alternative territorialities.

Territorial struggles, therefore, are not simply struggles for space. They are struggles for and through the emergence of new territorialities. It is in this context that we can understand the meaning of the Zapatista territory. "We might best characterize the Zapatista strategy, then, as the construction of another structure of relation between a newly produced collective subject and space – a new 'territoriality'" (Reyes 2015: 421). In this understanding of Zapatismo, Alvaro Reyes refers to a somewhat different notion of territoriality, borrowed from Claude Raffestin, according to which, "territoriality is the ensemble of relations that humans maintain with exteriority [the physical environment] and alterity [the social environment] (2012: 139). For Raffestin, territoriality is "the 'skeleton' of everyday life … the hidden dissimulated structure of the everyday" (2012: 129). Using this concept, Reyes arrives at a conclusion which is similar to the one suggested so far in this text, namely that territory is constructed as a process that shapes social relations and, thus, collective subjects.

"Alternative social rationalities" emerge in Zapatista communities because new forms of social organization and government are being tried out. This is a process that sustains a new way of practicing politics aimed at emancipatory changes. Such politics draws from the existing creative forces that give "those below" the power to survive despite dominant neoliberal policies of discrimination and "expulsion" (Sassen 2014). "[T]he Zapatistas propose that the politics of changing worlds requires the harnessing of the structures of value and social relations that are present below for the construction of organizational forces that would make possible the definitive exteriorization of those worlds from the world of capitalism (Reyes 2015: 419).

Whereas the "definitive exteriorization" is a defined scope (a "beyond" the capitalist relations and the statist forms of organizations), Zapatistas do not start from establishing such an exteriority in the form of an autonomous state separated from Mexico. They know that this state would soon be transformed into a precarious protectorate due to its limited resources and power (if it ever managed to successfully separate itself from the Mexican state, of course). On the other hand, they also know that their peculiar project of autonomy "inside Mexico," is really a form of reaffirming a territorial logic which is different from that of the real-existing neoliberal states. Mexico is perhaps one of the most extreme examples of the consequences of advanced neoliberal capitalism. The Mexican state territory is an arena of struggle between various rival capitalist centers of power (drug cartels and local political mafia included). Mexican territory is fragmented and fragmenting. Reclaiming territories and constructing new territorialities means, for Zapatistas, producing a different world "in, against, and beyond" the existing one (which is dangerously approaching humanity's survival critical margin).

In the context of such a project of social emancipation, shared spaces acquire a very important role. It is in those spaces that the reclaiming of new territorialities actually takes shape. In shared spaces, Zapatistas do not simply practice commoning as a form of regulating and producing egalitarian social relations. They produce in those spaces new collective subjects capable of mobilizing both ancestral traditions and new critical knowledges. New collective subjects are being shaped only through everyday practices in which new forms of coexistence are being developed, forms of coexistence that depart from the predatory capitalist ethos. A politics of culture is crucially important in such a project. Learning from the cultural politics of Latin American movements (including indigenous movements, feminist and queer

movements, rural movements, and landless and homeless movements), Zapatistas seem to have realized how important space
sharing is, not only as a means for their communities' survival but
also as a means for developing alternative values: collective and
personal dignity, equality, justice, solidarity, respect for difference
and plurality, participation in collective decisions. Their communities, therefore, actually territorialize a different emerging
culture which redefines democracy.

Zapatista building of autonomy in Chiapas may help us reformulate a controversial proposal connected to the resistances
against prevailing globalization's de-territorialization effects:
the reclaiming of place as opposed to the predominance of the
space of flows. As Arturo Escobar helps us understand, in their
"politics of the defense of place" (2001: 165) social movements
"are not just trapped in places" (2001: 166) but rather defend
"local models of nature and cultural practices" (2001: 163) while
actively and creatively engaging, at the same time, with translocal
forces, producing "novel politics of scale" (2001: 163).

So, if one wants to study the effects of Zapatista territorialized and territorializing politics, one needs to see how specific
forms of place making (and therefore, specific forms of space
sharing and commoning in and through space), indeed clash with
established territorialities (both those contained in the Mexican
state as well as those harnessed by globalization mechanisms).
Zapatista territory is a dense network of insurgent territorialities
that shape spaces of insurgent education, autonomous assemblies,
self-government, and the everydayness of commoning. Zapatista
territory is a socio-spatial mechanism which keeps on producing
within the Mexican territory (but also beyond that) dispersed,
and in many different ways interconnected, spatial nuclei of
emancipatory commoning.

A school in Chiapas

The construction of a school for Zapatistas educators (*promotores
de educación*) in a remote community in Lacandona rainforest
might appear as a minor example of commoning place-making
in Zapatista territory. Unfolding its history, however, we might

discover how rich, complex and indicative this process is if we are to explore the potentialities of an architecture of emancipating commoning in Chiapas.

It was in 2000 when a group of Greek activists and supporters of the Zapatistas uprising formed a collective named "A School for Chiapas Campaign." Their aim was to collect money and to actively participate in the construction of a school for teachers who were going to become the backbone of the emerging alternative education system in Zapatista communities. This project took its initial form through visits and discussions in Chiapas in the previous year, during which a design proposal by two students of the School of Architecture of National Technical University of Athens was submitted to autonomous Zapatista territories. According to this proposal, the "school" was actually envisaged as an extended educational community, comprising classrooms, dormitories and a collective kitchen, a library, a basketball ground, and various outdoor meeting places. Autonomous authorities, which had already described the needs and logic of this autonomous education center, approved the plans and decided to start the construction of the school in Culebra, a community belonging to the Autonomous Insurgent Municipality Ricardo Flores Magon.

From the very first step of this collective adventure the project was conceived as a collaboration between Greek and Mexican militants in support of the Zapatista cause, based on mutual trust, voluntary work and engagement, equality and shared enthusiasm for the struggle to establish an autonomous society. Building a bridge between worlds so far away from each other was not an easy task. It took two and a half years of effort to construct this school and during this time around 1000 Zapatista people as well as 120 Greeks volunteers (who went to Culebra in groups of 3 to 4 people) worked hard, not only with their hands and brains to solve innumerous problems but also with their hearts. Here is how a representative of the initiative described this collective experience of creating a common ground: "Long distances, long working days and long discussions traversed by curiosity and silence. Much to learn for both sides by talking, but also, not so rarely, by remaining silent, by extending steps, passages and bridges over ambiguities and eyes saying *I don't understand*, and then, *I get it now*, nurtured by difference and supported by dignity" (One School for Chiapas Greek Solidarity Group 2004).

This process of construction, thus, was not a simple technical or technological procedure in which people participated in pre-arranged and socially legitimized roles. People from both parts of the world had to invent the common ground in which they could first of all collaborate as construction workers: This was, in itself, not an easy task, given that Greeks had to learn and use local construction knowledge and that Lacandonias had to devise ways to materialize architectural forms, which were quite different from the ones they were used to, with available tools and skills. Commoning in the construction site was more than efficient collaboration, it was a cultural exchange, it was learning by working together, it was showing and giving respect.

Greek volunteers had to learn what it meant for their Chiapas comrades to walk one or even two days in the jungle in order to arrive to Culebra from "neighboring" communities and work in the school's building. And it was important for the Greeks to

3.2 Collective work in the construction site of Culebra school (Zapatista territory, Chiapas, Mexico)

realize that others in the home communities of the Zapatistas who came to Culebra would look after their families and take their place in their farming duties: collective work for a common cause manifesting itself in the unfolding of an everydayness based on mutuality and solidarity.

Everydayness in Culebra provided invaluable experiences to all those involved. At first, the Greeks were received with a kind of shy skepticism. Although their intentions were obvious – they arrived in order to help – their behavior was not always according to local *usos y costumbres* (customs and habits). Those communities, although willingly exposed to the external influences coming with the international solidarity initiatives, had to learn how to treat cultural differences and different patterns of practices. On the other side, Greeks carried with them, often unwillingly, cultural prejudices, which often survived under their leftist or anarchist ethics. They sometimes questioned choices made by the communities concerning, for example, the organization of agricultural production or the "efficiency" of certain construction choices. Some of the Greek volunteers had to fight against their culturally inculcated ideas connected to progress (projected on images of "backwardness") or to individual happiness (considered as distinct from common, shared happiness). As one Greek volunteer remarked: "Maybe Zapatistas have not developed necessary technologies, progress, means of production, knowledge production in general, maybe they merely 'collectivize their misery,' but this does not mean that their experience is bound to fail" (V. B., Greek volunteer).

On the other hand, everyday life in Culebra had standing effects on the Greek volunteers' views, values, and feelings. As most of them remember, collective dignity was the most important quality of common life pursued by the insurgent locals. You could see it in the eyes of the women who were struggling to make equality a real everyday experience. You could see it in the play of children who were free to enjoy life under the protection of the community, in stark contrast to the treatment of children of indigenous people in non-Zapatista areas, who have to work in the streets in dangerous and miserable conditions. You could see it in men and women who rotate in various community duties (including the cultivation of collectively owned community land, which in certain cases was land recuperated from *latifundios*). You could see it in the proud humbleness of the men and women who for only a short time become the elected representatives of their community: authorities that learn to "govern by obeying" (*mandar obedeciendo* is the Zapatista moto for "good government"). So, everyday mundane events acquire the character of examples of a different way to live in dignity. Those events sometimes become allegories of an ongoing re-invention of emancipatory politics.

As a volunteer remembers: "One day we were returning from the school's construction site. The day before we had one of those hard rains which turn every path to mud. Walking along the river we suddenly met an old blind man who was escorted by a young child who was helping him find his way. We said hello in a very friendly way that is so customary in this village. And then the old man said '*Ya no se ve el camino*' (One cannot see the road any more) ... Behind this short phrase (and the way it was uttered) is an authentic view of life that can be expressed with only one word (to which we keep on returning): dignity" (Z. Z., Greek volunteer). A blind individual is not blind any more if he is part of a community which tries to see with him. And although finding the road is difficult, it is something that no one alone is capable of doing.

As another Greek volunteer remarks: "something enormously important for me is that in Chiapas, in the languages that people speak, there is no word for 'I.' They always use [instead] the word 'we'" (S. P., Greek volunteer). By noticing such a difference between languages, which had to communicate through the intermediary use of Spanish (the language of the colonizers which both Greeks and Tzoltzil and Tzeltal people had to learn as a "foreign" language), one becomes aware of the commoning power of translation. It is by building the precarious bridges of translation (a practice we will explore in the next chapter) that a feeling of *communalidad* emerges. As Gustavo Esteva summarizes it, this feeling is actually expressed as a different "horizon of intelligibility: how you see and experience the world as a 'we'" (Esteva 2012).

The construction of the school, therefore, has activated prac-

tices of sharing spaces through creative encounters even before
the school itself was finished. A community's shared space, developed through the territorial struggles of the Zapatistas, became a
true testing ground of potential territorialities of solidarity due
to the interaction between the Greek volunteers and the Culebra
(and other communities) people. The process of construction
triggered experiences of cooperation and sharing that actually
prefigured the forms of encounter meant to unfold in the school-
community under construction.

It seems that in this project means were shaped by ends. The
process reflected the essential characteristics of the scope that
motivated it: a new liberating education that tries to encompass the wisdom and knowledge of different people in struggle
is essentially an osmotic education. Through its pores different
cultures communicate and cross-fertilize. Zapatistas never meant
to simply construct an indigenous particularism although they
explicitly supported the careful appropriation of Mayan traditions. Osmotic was the process of building the Culebra school too.
The construction site was actually a laboratory of sociocultural
experiments of cooperation. It was a threshold, a space between
two worlds so near and so far apart at the same time: an osmotic
space of encounters in which both "locals" and "foreigners" tested
the prejudices and discoveries of their traditions.

The spatial arrangement of this alternative insurgent education
environment and the actual choices of architectural forms were
also the means to express, as well as to facilitate, a different kind
of knowledge and collectivity: "We wanted not only a different
content of education but even a different form for the educational
process which takes place in the classrooms. We don't want in
these classrooms to see the backs of our comrades as happens
in the Government's schools. We want space to be different, so
that it permits us to see each other's face, to meet and know each
other. And these thoughts of ours coincided with the architectural
proposals that our Greek comrades presented us" (Julio, member
of the Autonomous Council of the Insurgent Municipality to
which Culebra village belongs, addressing the school's inauguration ceremony).

We know, of course, that different theories about education, from the most libertarian to the most traditionally hierarchical, have developed in recent history, putting extreme emphasis on the actual space they were to use. The school in Culebra was therefore designed with an awareness that the educational process is a process which takes place not simply in certain "spatial containers" but is actually space sensitive: available space may distort, promote, or encourage specific educational scopes. A school with circular (actually of hexagonal shape) classrooms is to host a non-hierarchical mode of sharing knowledge. Space form matters.

A careful researcher of ancient democracy, J.P. Vernant has explicitly documented the emblematic and functional importance of the spatiality of democratic deliberation: "It is significant that the expression *en koinoi*, whose political meaning, 'to make public, place in common,' has been mentioned, has a synonym with a clearly spatial meaning. Instead of saying that a question is put *en koinoi*, that it is debated publicly, it can be said that it is placed *en mesoi*, put in the center, set down in the middle" (2006: 206). In an emerging world of practiced democracy, the *agora* became the place of practiced equal participation but also pro-

3.3 A commoning education in a school produced through commoning (Zapatista territory, Chiapas, Mexico)

vided the emblematic image of such a practice: "Insofar as they have access to the circular space centered on the agora, citizens enter a political system governed by equilibrium, symmetry and reciprocity" (2006: 207).

The Culebra school classrooms, which were conceived according to an architectural tradition of anti-authoritarian school design, were meant to be commoning catalysts. In an emerging society of equality and solidarity, education is part of the construction of liberated communities. Education is for the community and develops critically both the needs and the knowledges of the community. Educational spaces, thus, are spaces of commoning, spaces in which education is shaped, developed, and used as commons: "For us real education means not to separate knowledge from our demands, not to separate education from our history, the history of our fathers and grandfathers, which teaches us how they cultivated land, how they fought their struggles, which teaches us how to struggle" (Zapatista *promotores de educación* addressing the inauguration ceremony).

Prominent at the center of the school's complex is the library building. As if to radiate an almost stubborn decisiveness to transcend the material and economic conditions of a village in Lacandona rainforest, this building is a lot more than a place for reading and storing books. It is a gesture, expressed in architectural form but also in practices of habitation, which directly reveals the meaning of Zapatista autonomy. Not a stronghold of enclosed otherness but, nevertheless, a bold affirmation that education, as well as society, can take forms which transcend existing capitalist relations.

A two-story building made of wood and cement blocks, with roofs that not only protect but also shine in the Mexican sun, it is a building that was not only difficult to construct but indeed expresses this difficulty: it is a collective achievement.

We are used to connecting pride with selfishness, the worst kind of individuality. Or we tend to connect it with national arrogance and heroic patriotism, which is always just a step away from racism and policies of exclusion. What if, however, there is a kind of collective pride connected to commoning? People may feel proud, not because they are different or better or because they

3.4 The Culebra school's library

are descendants of glorious ancestors, but because they manage to
collectively accomplish something that strengthens their common
aspirations without attacking or downgrading others. Pride, in
such a case, is a positive feeling of sharing, a feeling connected to
common dreams and to common efforts.

The school in Culebra has made many people proud. Many

have seen in the school's presence in the heart of Zapatista territory a proof that collaboration propelled by shared values can be an emancipatory process which produces tangible results. The school complex is a collective work, a product of sharing but also a means for sharing – sharing knowledge, sharing experiences, sharing ideas and questions. Collective pride makes it even more than that: it elevates it to the status of a proof: we can create collectively what we collectively decide is necessary in our effort to liberate ourselves form a social organization that destroys the lives of the many along with the planet itself. Sharing feelings, thus, can indeed be part of a commoning process.

A Mexican journalist, Hermann Bellinghausen (2004), compared this school in Chiapas with the project of creating an opera in the middle of the jungle, which was the theme of Herzog's well-known film *Fitzcarraldo* (1982). This project was conceived and partly executed with unbelievable determination and with almost surrealistic gestures in face of insurmountable difficulties and misfortunes. The school in Chiapas, however, managed to surpass all the obstacles and is firmly rooted in a community that uses and protects it. No matter how surrealistic the buildings seem in a village with humble wooden houses, no matter how beyond the actual means and resources of the community the maintenance of the complex is, this work is there to prove that collective dreams may become invincible.

4

Reclaiming public space as commons: the squares movement and its legacy

Between 2011 and 2013, an important kind of shared experience activated by the potentialization of public spaces became prominent in many cities throughout the world. What came to be named as the squares movement includes instances of the Arab Spring (especially in Tunis and Cairo), square occupations in Europe (in Madrid, Barcelona, London, Athens, and many more), Gezi Park mobilizations in Istanbul, Hong Kong "umbrella" demonstrations, and the Occupy movement (including Zucotti Park mobilizations).

This chapter attempts to sketch out a re-appraisal of the squares movement by focusing on characteristic forms of public space appropriation that may be considered to constitute examples of a new kind of space-sharing as well as a promising set of ways of sharing through space. It will be argued that space in the squares movement became a crucial factor in the shaping of dissident acts as well as those who planned and performed such acts. Space was potentialized through acts that inventively reclaimed the "public," while at the same time igniting processes of identity crisis experienced by those who participated in the mobilizations.

The core of the proposed argument establishes an interpretative analogy between actual changes (collectively imagined or projected ones) in occupied spaces and changes in the subjects of action (stemming from experienced identity crisis). The terms which will attempt to encompass and host this analogy, not unexpectedly, have an implicit or explicit spatial reference:

transposition, transformation, and translation. The prefix trans-, which those terms share, indicates a movement through space (considered either as an abstract or as a more concrete realm or medium), a crossing, a passage. As it will be shown, at the center of this analogy lies a very rich spatial metaphor, the metaphor of the threshold.

Transposition: visiting otherness

In its literal meaning transposition is an act (or a process) in which someone or something changes position in space. This spatial image is, of course, the basis of many metaphoric uses of the world (among them a change of key in music). Could one then suggest that participants in the squares movement occupations were transposed, that they were experiencing processes of transposition?

At the first level, people were indeed transposed in space. They were mobilized by their anger, by their needs, and by their dreams, to "take it to the streets." This expression indicates a kind of rupture in everyday routine trajectories (people are in places through which they normally simply pass), as well as an emphasis on the symbolic potentialities of public space rather than on its functional role in city-life. Transposition, in this case, does not simply mean being at a place which is different from the one that normally describes you but also being at a place which has acquired new characteristics exactly because you are transposed to it (the street as a protest stage).

We can possibly discern in the uses of the word, including the metaphoric ones, an important characteristic both of the act and the results of it: it is something that one may do to oneself. When we talk about people being transposed to the streets and to the squares we need to understand an act of intentionality on their part.

On a second level, transposition may describe an act that changes the characteristics of the acting subject due to the fact that it entails a change in place. Transposition may be used metaphorically to explain a change in behavior, a change of attitude, a shift in expressions. But, transposition does not necessarily lead

to a transformation. It is more like the result of a change in position which (theoretically or in practice) can be reversed. An actor
is transposed: Richard Schechner, the theoretician and founder
of performance studies, distinguishes between performances
in which "performers are returned to their starting places" (he
calls them transportations) and those in which performers are
changed in a more permanent way (he calls them transformations) (Schechner 1985: 125). "Acting, in most cases, is the art of
temporary transformation – not only the journey out but also the
return" (1985: 125).

In the occupied squares, a practice of transposition, which literally gave to people a place that they were not used to considering as their place, actually triggered a peculiar human capacity to
become other without losing oneself in otherness. This capacity,
due to which the art of theatricality becomes possible (Stavrides
2010: 81–96), makes people capable of visiting otherness.

Encounters between different types of people often took
place in the occupied squares without any pre-determined set of
encounter rules and collaboration habits. Such encounters established, or generated attempts to establish, innovative patterns of
communication and of collaboration and, thus, of commoning.
As common ground was not already there in the form of recognizable common interests or shared histories of collaboration; it
had to be developed in improvised performances of sharing and
through negotiations based on mutual respect. The process of
creating common ground does not simply involve agreements.
People explore, with all the means and capacities they have, the
potentialities produced by the de-facto co-presence of differences.

Transposition in this context involves the inhabiting of in-
between areas, thresholds. Visiting otherness, meeting others and
negotiating the common ground between the participants of the
squares movement means learning to construct this common
ground without eliminating the differences that actually shaped
the need for it.

Discussions on the distinction between the inherent power
of the multitude and the potentiality of individuation processes
which result in collaborating singularities may indeed offer us
important clues concerning the role of transposition experiences

in the context of the squares movement. Developed by Hardt and Negri, as well as by Virno and other theorists inspired by the Italian political thought of the 1970s, the term *multitude* tries to describe a new phase in the composition of the working classes. Based on the Marxian legacy according to which working conditions and relations of production actually shape the collective subjects which challenge capitalism, the multitude appears to be the specific form of collective subject which corresponds to the contemporary phase of this socio-economic system.

There seems to be a crucial interpretative problem at the center of the multitude argument that directly affects the understanding and "explanation" of the squares movement: The multitude is, at first glance, and as the term designates, an agglomerate of differences, an incoherent medley of trajectories, a plurality of overdetermined social roles. As Virno describes it, "Multitude is the form of social and political existence for the many, seen as being many," a "plurality which does not converge into a synthetic unity" (2004: 21–22). Is there, however, a shared characteristic behind such a diversity? And is this characteristic inherently present in the life of the multitude or is it the product of specific circumstances? Is the potential common ground of multitude's practices and multitude's forms of social existence constitutive of the multitude or is it a possibility triggered by certain performances and inhibited (or destroyed, postponed etc.) by certain other ones?

By studying the squares movement we can possibly extract some answers to the above question. People came to the squares and participated in the corresponding struggles by connecting to the squares' demands and aspirations through different channels. For many this was an opportunity to express their anger against injustice. For many, too, this was a case of experiencing the warmth of solidarity and of communal bonds. For some, their participation was directly linked to aspirations for a different society. And for others, this was one more occasion to claim specific rights that are in danger or completely effaced by harsh neoliberal policies (including rights connected to gender, culture, work, migration, and so on). Any attempt to describe this copresence at the squares in terms of a definite pre-existing social subjectivity is bound to fail.

The idea of a multitude populating the squares seems plausible. However, the process of transposition introduces a perspective that somehow shifts the ground underneath the questions posed. Those who participated in the squares movement obviously had social identities before they came to the squares. But the performative unfolding of the squares' events actually challenged the prescriptive character of those social identities and put into crisis established forms of habitus. Central to this process was a legitimization crisis. Those who came to the squares were doubtful, if not completely disillusioned, about the unifying (or unitary) rhetoric of neoliberalism. And since this was a period in which promises for a better life were not even given (let alone fulfilled) to large parts of the population (migrants, precarious workers, young professionals, heavily indebted households), many of the squares participants were actively (in a performative way) demanding a role and a voice from a society that was excluding them.

In the Arab region this meant a direct confrontation with autarchic governments. In the European cities it meant a direct clash with unjust and devastating austerity policies. In the Americas and Asia it meant a direct challenge to established economic oligarchies. In all cases however, delegitimization seems to have led to a reclaiming of democracy. We know, of course, that this term is at the center of fierce debates, and that it has become the ideological flagship of the self-proclaimed "free world." Ambiguities and direct contradictions may result (and indeed have resulted) from this pre-history of the term. However, the squares did not simply declare the importance of democracy but explicitly experimented with practices of democracy. This is one of the most important and long-standing legacies of those events. People were actually inspired to invent forms of democracy that would once again give the term its original meaning: "the rule of *demos*" (the people in Greek). And in all cases, they chose to experiment with "direct democracy" rather than with "representative democracy," which in many countries was connected to corrupt politicians and established oligarchies.

"Means should look like ends" seems to have been a guiding principle for the squares' organization, even if this formulation was not always explicitly stated. And this has heavily influenced both the squares movement legacy and the initiatives that were inspired by this legacy. Although ideological debates about the true meaning of democracy were in abundance during that period, collective experiences of democracy shaped both the key ideas and the practices which flourished in the occupied squares.

Far from being the result of spontaneous actions, these experiences of democracy actually produced, as well as tested, new forms of organization and collaboration. The Syntagma square occupation, for example, produced experiences of democracy-as-collaboration, both when people had to defend themselves from the violent attacks of police riot squads and during everyday discussions for the distribution of the square's maintenance tasks. Bodies experienced democracy as collaboration without a coordinating "outside" (a leading or decision-making group, a committee etc.).

If this, then, was a mobilization of multitudes, it was a mobilization that produced (rather than confirmed) a common ground. And this common ground was not simply reflected in practices of participation and collaboration which unfolded in the squares. It was literally created by them: the common ground *was* those practices.

We are accustomed to seeing, for example, assemblies as areas of deliberation, as debate arenas in which opposing views clash. And we seem to assume that what makes assemblies more democratic or more participatory than other forms of deliberation is the rules agreed upon (or even imposed by some) through which opinions are expressed and decisions are being taken. However, the square assemblies in many cases have shown that they provided something more than that: the ground for transpositions. They gave to participants the means and the opportunities to visit the otherness of others, to observe those whom they didn't notice before or those whose difference they didn't have the tools to understand before. Assemblies became arenas of exposure and crossroads of encounter trajectories. This was due to the fact that they were not assemblies summoned by an already established collectivity, as is a workers assembly, or a student assembly, or a leftists or anarchists assembly (a political assembly). The squares

4.1 Occupied Syntagma square in Athens (2011): the general assembly

assemblies, or smaller initiative-centered assemblies within the occupied squares, were actually areas in which identities and aspirations were not simply expressed but also re-shaped through transposing encounters.

Co-presence in the squares did not instigate a process of homogenization. In contrast to the idea that co-presence at work (and especially in factory workplaces) produces a homogeneity that may become the basis of collective resistance, co-presence in the squares shaped collective resistances based on heterogeneity. Co-presence gave different people the opportunity to construct a common ground that was always to be negotiated through participation in practices of collaboration, more like a collectively enacted in-betweenness than a place defined by its use. Syntagma square has a long particular history, being the central square of Athens, and dominant discourse connects its meaning with the Modern Greek state's national identity. This identity is firmly anchored in monumental landmarks (such as the Monument of the Unknown Soldier situated at the upper part of the square) and in the dominant presence of the Parliament building (initially built as the first king's palace). Public ceremonial space reflects a specific authority and its legitimizing myths. The performed common space of occupied Syntagma square, however, was not the locus of a recognizable identity. Less a place and more like an urban threshold, this common space was connecting the center of Athens with developing nodes of anti-austerity resistance. Syntagma became a porous space, a "territory in resistance," as defined in the previous chapter.

Whereas the factory represents a space of enforced collaboration, which Marx, among others, considers as an opportunity to develop in practice a shared conscience, the occupied square became the testing ground for various kinds of collaboration (not necessarily orchestrated by overarching decisions) that were chosen by the participants themselves in direct expression of their will to resist injustice and suppression. Coordinated actions, whether in the form of organized protest, or in the form of organized defense against police raids, or the attack of aggressive thugs (as in the case of Gezi or Tahrir occupations), were also not the result of a central planning committee, but were either directly decided upon in assemblies, which were counting on the different roles to be planned by existing or emerging collectivities, or through direct negotiations between different collectivities (with differing forms of internal homogenization). Thus, during the Syntagma occupation, it was the assembly that assigned different roles to different groups (some of them were formed as commissions during the occupation), whereas during the Cairo Tahrir occupation, militant football fans were legitimized to take on a decisive role in clashes with those who attacked the occupied square (Alexander 2011: 42) because they were representing a general will (although this will was not expressed in assembly decisions). It was those same groups that also organized the chains of people who protected the Cairo museum from looting. In the Gezi Park struggle, the coordination between different groups was not established through assembly decisions but was built through negotiations (immediate or mediated) in practice between people who before the occupation belonged to different or even directly hostile parts of the society (e.g. Kemalists, LGTB activists, Kurds, Besiktas football fans etc.).

Returning to assemblies as collective experiences of transposition, it is interesting to observe the decision-making process as a direct expression of transposition acts. In Syntagma square, for example, the decision taken to recognize the right for everybody to address the assembly was connected to the choice to draw a limited amount of lots that would determine who would actually take the stand and in what sequence (since it would be meaningless for an assembly to go on for hours and thus exclude all those who would need, for example, to go to work early the next day). This agreed-upon choice (Giovanopoulos and Mitropoulos 2011) did not only organize the decision-making process in a more efficient way; it performatively created equality and an interchangeability of roles. It was a mechanism that prevented the accumulation of power in the hands of the possibly more organized speaker groups or of those who had more free time or an accumulated activist experience.

Furthermore, chance determined in an arbitrary way the sequence of speakers. So, even though this procedure sometimes produced incoherencies or retrogressions in the process of deliberation, speakers gradually learned to focus their contribution on questions about a possible decision proposal (usually formulated by smaller working groups before the assembly) without feeling the need to be absolutely coherent, conclusive, and even convincing. This was an experience of a politics based on complementarity that sustains differences but builds bridges between them, rather than a politics aiming at homogenization. Indeed, in those experiences it was proven that, "The assembly as a political formation can provide both the means for beginning to seriously engage with the production of the common and the organizational terrain for the common politics to come" (Thorburn 2017: 70).

The labor of translation

Translation is a process that bears interesting similarities with transposition. Commenting on Benjamin's text on "The task of the translator," a text which will be referred to in this chapter,

Paul de Man observes that the German word for translation, "*uebersetzen* translates exactly the Greek *metaphorein*, to move over, *uebersetzen*, to put across" (1986: 83). The practice of translation is, in German, connected to an image of movement from one space to another. Similar is the term "metaphor" (coming directly from the Greek verb already mentioned), which is a trope also indicating a movement – from one context of meaning to another. In addition, the Spanish word for translation is *traduccion* and the French *traduction*. Both words come from the Latin *traducere* which means moving from one place to another.

Translation is a form of transposition. However, this passage from one meaningful context to another, from one language to another, is not simply a correspondence established in order to ensure that meaning passes swiftly from one side to the other. Walter Benjamin insists that translation of literary works is actually totally disengaged from the problem of a work's content, or meaning. To use de Man's careful translation of a crucial passage of this text: "So instead of making itself similar to the meaning, to the *Sinn* of the original, the translation must rather, lovingly and in detail, in its own language, form itself according to the manner of meaning [*Art des Meines*] of the original" (de Man 1986: 91).

Translation is a work on form, which attempts to create passages not from one language to another but from one work (the original) to another (not the copy but the translated). In Benjamin's reasoning it is important to distinguish the original and the translation, since the latter constitutes a product of the afterlife of the former (Benjamin 1992b: 72). However, if we choose to observe acts of translation between speaking subjects, then translation may travel both ways, each time defining the different original as merely a point of reference. Translations, thus understood, create passages between constituted differences. What motivates the creation of these passages is a firmly established belief that there is a common ground which differences sometimes hide. Maybe this belief in language communication is the belief in the specificity of meaning regardless of the form used to convey it. People try to bypass the obstacle of difference in order to establish this common ground. And being reassured that you attribute the same meaning to something with others, that you share meaning, is an extremely gratifying sentiment.

However, as our daily experience of communication shows, meaning is often elusive, difficult to be sure about, painfully fleeting and, at times, surprisingly absent. Translation is more like an incessant labor to establish connections, passages that will facilitate the creation of a precarious common ground. What is rightly termed as the "labor of translation" (Mezzadra and Neilson 2013: 243) is an ongoing process and involves: "a discourse of foreigner to foreigner which creates a language that is common precisely because it is forever in translation, and rooted in material practices of cooperation, organization and struggle" (2013: 275).

Translation, instead of affirming and gesturing towards a pre-existing common, a transparency of meaning allegedly polluted by the curse of difference (the Babel punishment), is actually producing the common. It is an act of creating the common by accepting that differences will never be overcome in an ideal state of complete communication and total agreement. Collaborating in view of a mutually accepted scope, experiencing recognizable shared feelings of pain or joy (2013: 276), and communicating by sharing patterns of doing is an important substratum for translation practices.

The labor of translation is based on the sharing of experiences and on acting together. At the same time, it is this kind of labor that makes the acting in concert really possible, since it produces the ground for experiences to be compared and thus shared. Translation is an integral part of the labor of commoning, if commoning is not understood as an effort to establish homogenization. Translation becomes a process of commoning when shared meanings are developed because of differences and not in spite of differences.

According to Clara Rivas Alonso, urban movements that actively struggled for the right to the city of the urban poor (who were evicted from their neighborhoods by Istanbul urban renewal projects) "have contributed to new understandings of urban citizenship and solidarity that do away with those imposed borders defined by the combination of neoliberal agenda with identity politics" (Rivas Alonso 2015: 239). This is another way of saying that urban struggles actively challenge dominant citizen classifications and the resulting exclusionary, stigmatizing and victimizing policies. No matter how strongly market tendencies promote diversification and consumerist plurality, rules of dominant identity ordering (spatial identities included) are necessary for the preservation of the dominant characteristics of capitalist society.

Struggles, thus, not only confront imposed rules of normalization-through-homogenization but also challenge borders erected between those who may potentially share common worlds. If urban citizenship is more or less linked to a set of rights (concretized differently in different historic contingencies), solidarity seems to be the force that ignites the sparks of translation. Solidarity is a practice that recognizes common aspirations or needs but, perhaps deeper than that, creates relations based on practices of offering. And usually, if not always, solidarity is based on the convergence of practices coming from different spaces and sectors of social life. In solidarity, an offer starts a bridge of communication. And this bridge commences an act of translation.

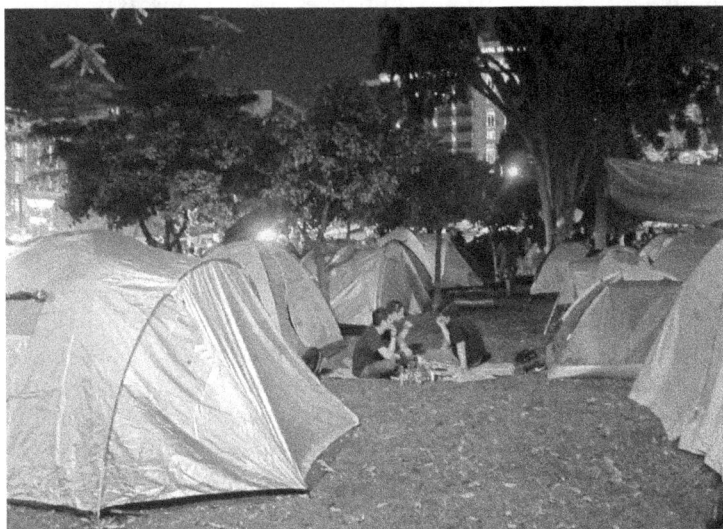

4.2 Occupied Syntagma square in Athens (2011): the tent city

The squares movement's tent cities became the expression of a collective will to explore new forms of life-in-common. It is here that we must locate the most enduring impact of the squares' experience. By developing patterns of collaboration in order to be able to maintain a kind of shared space that admits new-comers and encourages the expression of different life values as long as they accept the scopes of sharing, the occupied squares showed that solidarity may produce new habits and rules of living together.

Common space has been rediscovered after the Syntagma square occupation in lots of initiatives concerning efforts to resist the devastating effects of a socio-economic crisis. Self-managed health clinics, collective kitchens cooking for the poor, self-managed social centers and neighborhood cultural and educa-tional initiatives have spread all over Athens, all over Greece. All those initiatives develop their own way of sharing space, resources, and services produced by active participants (Stavrides 2016: 165–167).

The Social Cultural Center of Byron neighborhood in Athens, named "Lampidona" ("radiance" in Greek) is a characteristic example of post-Syntagma initiatives. Lampidona was "estab-lished in order to contribute to the unfolding of solidarity, creativ-ity and collective demands of the neighborhood's residents," as is explicitly stated in a manifesto declaration made in 2011. A richly diverse group of people describes with these words their common approach to the prefigurative aspirations of their actions:

> We want open public spaces of encounter, spaces in which we organize our common needs, our common demands, our shared struggles, spaces to discuss and create … We want this center to become a workshop for testing new kinds of relations opposed to the dominant ones. Relations which challenge the dominating commodification logic, which fight against the idea that those in the parliament will do what only movements can, relations which attempt to combine joyous gratification with the will to act, and, generally test today elements of the coming society we envision.

This is the kind of dynamics common space may activate. Common space is an everyday space and, at the same time, a space full of people's dreams for a just society, for life with meaning and dignity.

It is the same bridging process of translation that made it possible for the inhabitants of the Greek islands to host refugees who came to their land crossing the Aegean. Especially since 2015 onwards, and mainly due to the devastating war in Syria, desperate people choose to cross a rough and dangerous sea "illegally," and by using precarious means of transportation, in hope of a better future in Europe (disastrous shipwrecks often cause the loss of many lives). Islanders translated, through solidarity, the drama of the refugees to their own memories of migration, as well as to their own experiences of a devastating economic crisis. Such acts of translation-based practices were at the center of the squares movement, which is why they may be considered as one of its most important legacies. It was the Syntagma occupation spirit that re-emerged in the occupied self-managed centers for the refugees in Mytilini, Athens, and Thesaloniki.

Returning to Istanbul, the "Gezi Park Commune," this short-lived tent city (Karasulu 2015), in which so many different people met, was truly a declaration in practice of "the ability of the urban mass to do away with the historical construction of otherness that has been a constituent element of Turkish politics" (Rivas Alonso 2015: 240).

Experiences of transformation

If transposition is a process of visiting otherness, and translation a process of building bridges between different forms of otherness, transformation is becoming other. Whereas in transposition and translation the place of the other (literally as well as metaphorically) pre-exists the processes described, transformation may actually be directed towards an otherness in the making. To transform oneself or an existing space does not necessarily presuppose a self or a place that pre-exists as a model. In other words, if transposition is related to the art of theatricality, and translation related to the art of establishing correspondences (and to the art of translation as a literary genre), transformation is perhaps the art of creative exploration of change. It is a creative work on form which also, in terms of the underlying spatial meaning of the prefix trans-, gestures towards a displacement, a change in place which creates a place.

In transformation lurks the promise of the new, the promise of the different-as-new. Prefigurative elements may color the process of transformation. However, prefiguration in many cases appears as a process based on what Victor Turner (and Richard Schechner) called the "subjunctive mood" (Turner 1986: 42): "what if" things were different, what if capitalism did not dominate our lives and feelings, what if men and women were equal, and so on. Transformation is not limited by this "as if" (based on the "what if" taken as presupposition), which in a way marks a point of return (the return as a possibility that, as we saw, is connected to transposition). Transformation rather marks a point of no return. Thus, although it is not necessarily trapped in a modernist fundamentalism (always after absolute innovation), transformation gestures towards a beyond which is made actual. Transformation prefigures but also institutes, makes real a possible otherness (including the otherness of a different identity, a different future or a differently shaped space).

Did we have experiences of transformation in the squares? Could such experiences be connected to the production of shared identities or to the production of shared spaces? Transposition practices had important transformative effects on the occupied public spaces. In most of the cases tent cities became alternative urban microcosms, with many of the established functions of an urban cohabitation environment being recast in a new spatial form. The fact that those microcosms were under siege by the police or by other state-related forces (including government thugs in Cairo and Gezi) forced them to construct themselves as temporary. However, such alternative micro-cities indeed transformed existing public spaces and produced concrete examples of spatial arrangements that hosted and expressed a commoning culture.

The squares legacy and dissident creativity

To observe the transformative processes and results the squares movement culture had, it is helpful to compare two cases of occupied and reused hotels, one in Madrid and one in Athens, which epitomize the movement's creative legacy. The first was directly linked to 15M movement actions, which took place in the same year that the *indignados* occupied Madrid's Puerta de Sol, while the second was the result of movement actions in solidarity with refugees coming to Athens in the huge wave of 2015.

Hotel Madrid was occupied in October 2011, after a massive demonstration which took place in the adjacent Puerta de Sol. An ad hoc assembly decided, in the midst of a collective effervescence, to claim the building that had remained abandoned for a long time. According to the next day's communique: "We are a group of people who found an open and abandoned space but in a very good condition … We have decided to take it and to make it of social use" (Hotel Madrid 2011). Underlining the fact that the building belonged to a well-known land speculating company which "forms part of the economic mentality" that had resulted in the d crisis in the country, they declared: "It is for this reason that the liberation of the spaces which were usurped through this activity is completely legitimate" (Hotel Madrid 2011).

The terms used to describe the action taken were "recovery" and "liberation" (Abellán et al. 2012). Thus "the building was considered not only an autonomous and self-organized space, but also a meeting place for everyone, including neighbors and visitors (323). From the start, this "indiscriminate open-doors policy" (Shulman 2012) established an important, albeit not always easy to control, transformative potential in the shared life developed inside the building. The spatial arrangement which characterizes a hotel is usually based on very clear-cut demarcations of private spaces (the rooms), and facilities and spaces to be used by visitors and inhabitants under specific rules imposed and maintained by the management. This strict hierarchy of spaces was completely transformed by the occupation: two floors were arranged to mainly accommodate evicted families and the two remaining "were appropriated as space for the different working groups and assemblies, most of them constituted in the aftermath of protest camps" (Abellán et al. 2012: 324) The dynamics of this endeavor "also created a new series of groups and projects" (324). The osmotic relations between the projects and the people created a different space altogether inside the shell of a former hotel. Transformation was sometimes actual, material, but in most of the cases was instigated through a rearrangement of the meaning of spatial relations through sharing actions. "A laboratory of urban resistance" (324) it was, but at the same time it produced real changes in the lives and experiences of people involved.

Being able to maintain processes of collaborative cohabitation was not an easy task. This was "a super diverse group of people … with a mix of intentions" (Shulman 2012), including homeless and highly educated young activists. Sharing and living together needed rules to be devised, logistical issues (including organizing a collective kitchen) to be solved, and a security committee to be set up. Amidst all these difficulties, Hotel Madrid became a trans-formed and transformative space, shaping people who attempted to collectively shape it according to an ethics of sharing. "It wasn't perfect but it was *convivencia*, a Spanish word that can be translated as 'living together' of 'fellowship' in a secular sense" (Shulman 2012) is how a participant describes this experience. The fact that homeless or evicted people and middle-class activ-ists worked together, revealing to each other the potentialities and drawbacks related to their socially inculcated attitudes while going beyond them, proves that transformation processes were unfolding. But they were abruptly destroyed by the police, who evacuated the building after almost two months of creative explo-rations in shared life.

The ongoing project of the City Plaza self-managed Refugees Accommodation Center in Athens is a highly instructive relevant example. Established in April 2016 by groups of left activists and a group of refugees, this center is a squat in a central neighborhood of Athens, which gave new life to an unused hotel. The squat is organized into different groups (which also include international volunteers), which manage to provide a shared home for refugees seeking asylum in Europe in search of a decent life (a right they are being alienated from due to wars and economic disaster in their countries).

In terms of organization, this project clearly reveals the poten-tiality of identity transformation ignited by the coexistence of people from different countries and cultures, with different

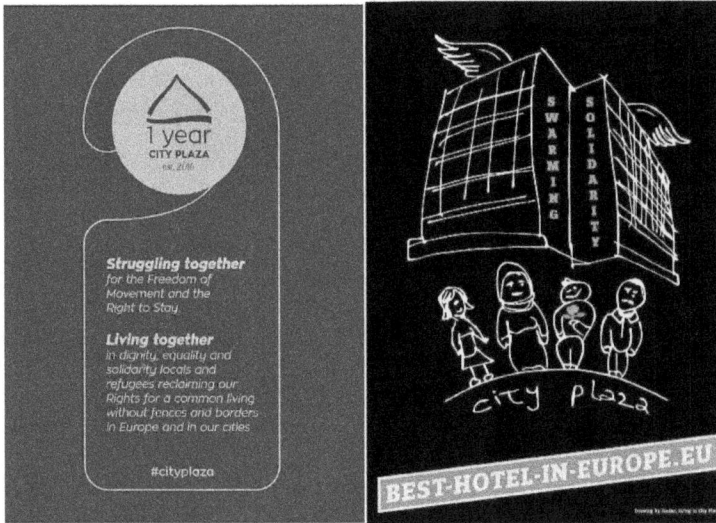

4.3 City Plaza: "Best hotel in Europe"

languages and religions, and with different needs (connected to their life histories and aspirations) but comparable longings. In order for this group of people (around 400) to be able to establish relations of cohabitation and collaboration within it, translation, in its literal meaning of establishing correspondences between different languages, is obviously needed. Translation, however, becomes a more complex process when those correspondences are being established (or, rather, created) through participation in shared duties and tasks. Thus, the collective evaluation and differentiated attribution of personal, family, or group needs is not a matter of efficient management based on the rational use of resources (coming from in-kind donations and from money contributions) but a participatory process involving long discussions.

This is actually a process of translations which take place at different levels of exchange. Through such exchanges a common ground based on the idea that participants are equal is established, needs are defined (e.g. the needs of children as different from the needs of adults), family bonds and different cultural and religious traditions are respected, and existing skills and developing

4.4 Inside the City Plaza occupied hotel in Athens

skills are mobilized for the common good. Translation, therefore, becomes a process which fuels everyday transformative
experiences.

Common space in City Plaza emerged through such multilevel
practices of translation in which the definition of intermediary
zones of common life use is being negotiated. Doors have been
removed from hotel rooms so that the areas of privacy are marked
by soft barriers (curtains) and thus potentially remain spaces connected to a shared "house" (refugees themselves actually refer
to City Plaza as their house). So it is not uncommon to see the
corridors as an extension of the collectively private space of an
extended family as well as spontaneous gathering spaces for the
"neighbors" of adjacent rooms. The rigidly departmentalized
space of the hotel was transformed into a network of differentiated areas of shared use, through the collective building of rules
and habits of sharing as well as by osmotic cross-fertilizations
of different temporalities (and rhythms) of co-presence and
collaboration. If, on the one hand translation ensures the organi-

zational efficiency needed for a collective kitchen that prepares meals for everybody (in which many alternate in duties), on the other hand ad hoc encounters and intentional relations between the dwellers create new relations which change people. Creative challenges to established views and preferences form in practice, and because of the developing results of space commoning, so do interesting identity juxtapositions and even hybridities. When a housewife who has learned how to cook, and used to cook for her family, becomes a member of the collective kitchen group, she transcends the boundaries of her traditional role: through commoning experiences family ties or religious and ethnic group ties become transformed from group enclosure defense mechanisms (even more so in periods of crisis) to constituents of large mutual help networks. Commoning in City Plaza helps people to transcend racist, ethnic, gender, or sexual behavior prejudices in a period in which dominant policies greatly promote hostility and xenophobia.

Appropriating public space and using it as a platform for protest has long been a practice of those who struggle for their rights or try to protect their collective interests. It was not only the poor and the disenfranchised that created such acts. Mobilizations targeting progressive governments or, in some cases, outwardly racist demonstrations were also orchestrated through public space appropriation. What seems to be a distinguishing characteristic of potentially emancipating struggles in and through public spaces is their power to activate popular inventiveness and participation. Being part of a large crowd in protest is usually consoling and gratifying; it can even make people feel that they belong to a powerful machine, a mighty war machine. These feelings, however, do not necessarily lead to liberating empowerment. Unless connected to mechanisms of sharing and equality, collective force may well lead to the consolidation of power imbalances, which, as we know, create hierarchies and subjection.

Maybe the squares movement and its legacy can teach us an important lesson on sharing. If sharing, or the feeling of belonging to a community of sharing, is not connected to rules and organizational forms that prevent the accumulation of power, then sharing can contribute to the establishment (or strengthening) of inequalities and the proliferation of enclosures. No matter how precarious and contradictory the practice of inclusiveness may be (focused on accepting newcomers and the otherness they constitute), it is an important prerequisite for efforts to challenge current exclusionary policies imposed by state apparatuses and market mechanisms alike.

Processes of transposition, translation, and transformation permeated the squares and after-the-squares collective experiences of creative resistance. What those processes share and encourage is collective inventiveness. And such inventiveness may be unevenly developed, sometimes in ways that do not necessarily add up to a major collective coordination of resistance acts. Nevertheless, inventiveness unleashes the creativity of people in action. And this creativity does not stem only from shared experiences connected to labor but also has to do with play, affective relations, innovative forms of criticism (including derisory acts and words targeting the powerful ones). Maybe creativity of this kind gestures towards the liberating power of doing released from obligatory and exploitative work, as Holloway seems to suggest (2002, 2010).

The Syntagma square occupation indeed generated an explosion of creativity and cultural production. Ad hoc feasts, the sharing of music and singing as well as improvised theatrical acts and happenings were part of the occupied square's everydayness. One interesting detail (that may have characterized other occupied squares too) is the way those cultural events contributed not only to the dissemination of the movement's demands and aspirations but also to the movement's own protection from police violence.

Police riot squads attacked the square on various occasions and with different "official excuses" ("obstructing circulation," "damages to public property," "imminent criminal behavior" etc.). In many cases, cultural creations and artistic performances became the means to organize resistance to such attacks, to keep the spirit high and, more than once, even to intercept police aggressiveness by ridiculing the invaders who had to face drums and songs instead of stones and *molotovs*.

Beyond the often paralyzing dilemmas of counter-violence

(against police brutality) versus "pacifism" lies another option: to immobilize mechanisms of state violence through mockery and festive collective acts which destroy the official rhetoric that presents state aggressiveness as necessary law-enforcement tactics in defense of "public security." Such inventive acts may be connected to the long tradition of charivari-like performances (Thompson 1993), which have often expressed the resistance spirit of "those below," while avoiding, simultaneously, disastrous confrontations with stronger opponents.

Much of the struggle tactics of the squares movement was based on the participation of people, on the enthusiasm generated from collective coordination and on the creativity unleashed by acts of disobedience. Tactics were discussed in the Syntagma square assembly as in many other square occupations. But there was always space for improvisation and, often, innovative acts of dissemination and resistance became catalysts for new collective initiatives. It is this spirit of emerging popular creativity, combined with a growing distrust for the "authorities," that has been circulating in society as a peculiar "regenerating virus" ever since. Militant activists usually observe societies in search for acts of insubordination, in search for major events that appear to inflict major changes. Maybe, however, ruptures in history only express changes that are being developing tacitly – often below the radar of dominant media – in everyday acts that, seemingly, only breed consent and obedience. If the Syntagma square occupation was indeed a surprise, this is not because it came from nowhere completely bypassing established politics (dissident politics included), but because those who consider themselves engaged in the struggle for human emancipation don't pay attention to minor events of discontent, to molecular acts of resistance, and to aspirations for a more just society that often punctuate people's everydayness. Thus, if we want to trace the potentialities released by the squares movement we need to abandon the erroneous clear-cut dichotomy between dissent and normality. These movements have indeed subverted the normalization process necessarily connected to the mechanisms of power (Foucault 2009). But they have done something more than that. Something which is less easily traceable. They have shown that our lives can be otherwise, that collaboration may produce humane relations and joy. That "we are many" and those who destroy our lives are very few. The delegitimization of power, the demythologizing of state violence, and the revelation of injustices did not result in the paralyzing view that nothing can be done, that politics stinks, that the powerful are invincible. Squares produced real tangible alternatives – to politics, to the everyday survival tactics, and to the existing forms of social organization. And those alternatives are bound to breed new eruptions of collective inventive resistance.

Many have studied this creative power of resistance, and some have connected it to a specific wisdom of the weak in face of asymmetrical power relations. Michel de Certeau saw in differentiations indicating "styles of use" the possible ground of deviation and resistance (1984). Marcel Detienne and Jean-Pierre Vernant studied *metis*, this peculiar multiple wisdom which helps the powerless to take advantage of opportunities in order to reverse power dy-symmetries (1991). Jan-François Lyotard used the example of the Sophists to indicate a form of reasoning that may become a weapon of the weak (1993). James Scott, who studied the "arts of not being governed" (2009), carefully observed the ways that the dominated used to avoid the results of subjugation through ingenious, albeit often camouflaged, acts of resistance. And Virno (2008), as well as Hardt and Negri (2005, 2009), has located in the multitude a rich repertoire of resistance tactics which are connected with innovative practices of organization.

What all those thinkers seem to suggest, albeit in very different theoretical contexts, is that inventiveness in action and thought should neither be connected to prominent individuals (politicians, artists, leaders etc.) nor to exemplary acts, but to a kind of metastatic, shared intelligence combined with a shared capacity to develop out of common experiences acts and practices which challenge existing norms and forms of life. The creativity of sharing is based on a shared creativity that is always further developed through sharing as an ever expanding creative process.

Interview with Zeyno Perkunlu, artist and member of the Müştereklerimiz (Our Commons) group which participated actively in the Gezi Park occupation (Istanbul 2013), 22 September 2016

Public space, common space

How was public space appropriated and transformed in the Gezi Park occupation? Were there specific forms of collective decision-making connected to the creation and maintenance of this shared space?

The answer to this question varies depending on the different moments of the protests. The roots of imagining Gezi Park as "our" public space (or reclaiming it) go almost a year back from the occupation when the pedestrianisation project of Taksim Square was announced by the municipality. Destroying the park, and building a shopping mall in its place, was part of a bigger urban plan. The people opposing the project organized protests of different forms: marching, petition campaigns, and law suits demanding the suspension of the municipality's decision etc. But in my opinion the most effective ones were the festivals organized in the park. During these events people re-discovered the park as a space where they can gather with friends in the form of a picnic while participating in protest actions, a space where they can socialize in the open air while listening to concerts. The first steps leading to the occupation were taken in those temporary appropriations of the space.

So when the project finally started, when the bulldozers entered the park to tear down the trees, people were already feeling engaged with the space on a different level. They had their memory of festivities and they knew the logistics of the park. But of course the people mentioned above were the ones who were already engaged with (in a very loose sense) political groups. The masses only engaged with this struggle after the uprising.

On the first three days of the resistance (28–31 May), the occupation was poorly organized. As the police were attacking every night and as they confiscated the materials in every raid, putting up tents in the park was a precarious endeavor. The tents were either symbolic or they were just used by people to spend the night.

On the 1st of June, in the afternoon after a night and a day of uprising, the police receded and opened the blockage of the park. From that moment on, a more organized occupation started. The crowd in the park was increasing every day. Some (already) organized groups started to organize the distribution of necessary provisions (blankets, tents, food, medical supplements), as well as a kitchen, a stage etc. But the "things to do" list and the number of decisions taken grew with the population of the occupation. The things that these groups could not anticipate were expressed by other people and more experienced protesters were encouraging the less experienced ones to take initiatives. Many friend circles or people who met in the park with similar wishes started to assume responsibilities in the organization of the occupation.

These initiatives were tied together via coordination desks. And most of the desks were formed through already existing networks. But the networks were also expanding with new participants. As the park occupation grew some maps were prepared to show "where to find what kind of services" or "which tent is responsible for what."

Taksim Solidarity Platform (Which was formed when the project started almost 1 and a half years before the occupation) also expanded during the occupation and became the organizer of the meetings where decisions were being taken. Around the end of the first week of the occupation, there were neighborhoods and streets inside the park (people named the paths between the tents and created districts) and each district was organizing its own assembly in order to send their ideas and discussions to the Solidarity Platform.

So in a way, both "already" organized groups and networks

and self-organized people formed the organization of the shared space.

(To make it more understandable I will just give an example: I was working in one of the coordination desks, which was formed by our network "Müştereklerimiz." One day a group of young women came to the desk and said "There are some men harassing women in the park, could 'you' do something about it?" We said: "Why don't you form an anti-harassment team? What we can do is to announce a meeting for women who want to participate in it. And you can go to feminist block and LGBT block's tents and ask their opinion." In a couple of days, the question "could you?" became "we are doing this" and people started to come by the desk not to ask but just to let us know. And we were passing the new initiatives information to Taksim Solidarity Platform.

Is it important to develop different forms of public space?
Definitely. Many times, when people are talking about the Gezi Resistance they say "It just happened." Which is true on a certain level. Nobody was expecting it. But this doesn't mean people weren't getting prepared for it or that some memories didn't help us imagine this possibility. I am not only talking about Tahrir or Syntagma or Puerta del Sol as the recent international experiences but also very local ones.

Just to mention two important ones: In 2010, Tekel factory workers went on strike. Realizing that there was a need for extra pressure in order for their demands to be accepted, they occupied one of the main streets of Ankara. This occupation lasted for months, causing a temporary new tent village in the middle of Ankara formed by workers and their families. In the same year, the protest for Emek Movie Theater's demolition had started and the protesters occupied the street of the theater periodically to show movies, give concerts, to cook and eat together. The Emek Movie Theater is a movie theatre located in the historical Serki Doryan building in the Beyoğlu district of Istanbul, which used to host the opening ceremony of the Istanbul Film Festival. The building had also been used in the 1970s and 1980s for secret 1st of May celebrations since they were prohibited by the government. In 2009, under the guise of renovation, a decision was given to demolish the building. These protests lasted for 3 years.

In both protests the creation and use of a new public space gave us the means to imagine new forms of struggle. So yes, a new form always brings new imaginations and new imaginations make possible new forms in the future.

On the other hand, as I mentioned in the answer to the first question, new forms of space create a mental jump in the participants. Physical togetherness in the space, sharing the same cause, and engaging with each other in a communal way creates new relational forms. And the new relational forms make it easier for people to take more initiative and act on their wishes and ideas.

Do you see any difference between public and communal space?
Yes. A public space could be used by public without any participation or without questioning any existing rules or meanings of the space. But a communal space (at least ideally) changes and challenges the space; it creates new means of relationalities.

Please refer to some crucial events that shaped your views about public space in contemporary metropolises (a reference to your organization's experiences and views would be very helpful in this context).
I have mentioned two important events in the first question. Both started in 2010. Tekel Workers Resistance was a long-lasting occupation which created its own space, and this shared space gave the workers more courage to resist for longer periods. My group was not part of it (it was the workers initiative) but many of us visited the workers camp and were inspired by it.

Although it began before our network's formation, we were more actively engaged with the Emek Movie Theater Resistance. In these protests collective use was emphasized against the commodification of our living spaces and the wounds opened in issues such as space, memory, and history; in the long run, this emphasis turned into one of the remnants of the social struggles after the Gezi uprising. The emphasis on the value of collective use suggested that the term "public" should not be defined only in relation to the state and that we, as users of the common, can redefine the "public." This paved the way for the first discussions on collective commoning, the results of which have been gradually seen in the Gezi Uprising.

(The Theater was demolished in the end but in the long run the tools of this protest were passed on to Gezi.)

What does it mean for you to share space? What is the meaning of private space for you?

Private space is a shifty term for me. Anywhere I can be alone when I need to that may provide basic comforts and satisfy needs can be a private space. It doesn't have to be owned yet it is also indispensable.

For me the important point about sharing a space is the possibilities that are not imagined beforehand. Bringing together people who share similar wishes to share a space often surprises us with new possibilities of organizing.

Recently, just a year ago, we started a shared, solidarity space for freelance workers. The idea behind it was to create a space for freelance workers that are usually isolated in their houses or in cafes that they use as temporary offices. Freelance work is often defined by the word "free" but we wanted to bring people together in order to discuss the exploitation processes in it.

Sharing the space produced several results. People sharing the space started to discuss the possibility of a translators' cooperative. They have started workshops to discuss their ways of dealing with freelance work's exploitation. And an unexpected result was the use of the space for forming a shopping cooperative in solidarity with Istanbul's historical city gardens.

Community

How did the Gezi community organize itself? Are we talking about a stable community, an expanding, dispersed or multi-polar community?

I think I have partly answered this within the first question. But to summarize again, it was a constantly changing community and also the organizational tools of it changed in time as well.

In many ways the Gezi community organized itself. But I

would feel unjust if I don't mention many grassroots organizations and groups who had patiently created and legitimized certain tools and the language of protests in the previous years leading to the Gezi Resistance. These groups had already opted for forms of free, horizontal, and anti-authoritarian organization, but within the process two important ideas – collectivity and the reaching out to the masses while remaining anonymous – were especially important. In many protests, festivals, and campaigns these tools were introduced and they were easily adopted by the masses during the Gezi occupation.

(I was recently in Kyiv and had the chance to discuss their experience in the Maidan uprising and saw the difference. Although the protest was initiated by university students, the lack of similar tools as well as the lack of protest history meant, as a result, the easy assimilation of the uprising by mainstream opposition parties. Because of this, many grassroots organizations left the occupation after the first couple of days.)

On the other hand, ideologically the community in Gezi was multi-polar. Everybody was there with their own agenda yet somehow converging in certain points.

Please describe the ways the Gezi movements have approached the problem of social inequality. Do you think that inequality is being shaped differently in cities than in rural areas? Is there any meaning for you in the term "spatial justice"?
First of all I am not really sure if we can say the Gezi Resistance became a movement. It has left many descendents but it is hard to define them as movements.

So I prefer to answer this question from my network's perspective.

From the beginning in 2009, when we were loosely tied to each other as different political groups, we aimed to emphasize that urban struggle is not distinct from flexibilization and precarization of labor, and that the control over common spaces in cities creates and sustains precariousness. What we learned is that urban struggle cannot be considered only in terms of physical transformation but urban transformation is also a political strategy that determines how people relate to each other. The precarious structures which make it impossible for people to organize work go hand in hand with the work environments and living areas which make it almost impossible for people to communicate with each other. For that reason, imagining a way out that is different from the forms of organization and resistance that we know and have gotten used to, was a necessity.

Our efforts were less connected to struggles in rural areas but through ecological groups we had some connection. We always tried to emphasize that the dispossession processes are the results of the same neoliberal policies both in rural and urban areas.

Did participating people collectively draw examples for self-management from shared traditions? Is collective memory a source for social experiments of collaboration? In what way?
I can't really think of local/cultural traditions that shaped self-management practices. But more political traditions were present. There were 5 main roads leading to Gezi Park and we knew which organization built which barricade in which street. So it was a common joke: "this barricade is more reliable than the other because this organization built it." It was a political joke about the acquired experience of some movements to build barricades and to clash with the police.

I would say I have seen more traditional jokes in the humorous side of the resistance. When Tayip Erdoğan called out to the mothers from TV saying; "Call your kids to return home, these protests should stop," many mothers came to the park with their slippers in their hands. It is a common tradition for mothers to throw slippers at their kids when they are angry. But this time they were showing the slippers to the president as a way of saying "we stand by our kids." I think these humorous traditions helped people to keep their morale up.

Just after the crowd was kicked out of the park and the police took control of the area, the Ramadan fasting period started. And with a call from the group "Anti-Capitalist Muslims," people started to celebrate the end of the fasting period together on the streets as crowded groups. These events were called "Tables of the Earth." Many protesters didn't even fast. The crowded dinners in the middle of Istiklal Street were a total confusion for the police. It was a religious act so they couldn't attack it and it gave people the opportunity to come together again despite police oppression.

Sharing and commoning

Do you think it is important to develop practices of sharing in and through space? How?
I think I have answered this question where I explain the freelance workers' solidarity space.

But to summarize, I have witnessed many occasions in which sharing a space or developing some practices for a specific place makes you realize common ideas or common discontents that you didn't even know existed. It helps people to express themselves, to become aware that they have common problems and to try to find ways to deal with them.

But of course I have also witnessed cases in which the fetishizing of shared space leads to closed and conservative communities. So space is important to try new forms and new relationalities but it shouldn't become the ultimate scope and/or the way a community become fascinated with itself.

Did the forms of participation in movement decision-making result in the rethinking and reshaping of the relation between public, communal, and private space?
Definitely. When the occupation was ended by police force, the public's first reaction was to continue organizing assemblies in their own neighborhoods, often in the neighborhood parks. During the first couple of months there were at least 60 assemblies in 60 different parks and most of them ended up calling themselves Neighborhood Solidarity Platforms.

Some of the Solidarity Platforms also started searching for assembly spaces during the winter: some of them occupied abandoned buildings and some forced the municipalities to give space to the neighborhood platforms. From that moment on, people started to be more engaged with the politics of their localities and even though many Neighborhood Solidarity Platforms disappeared in time, the loose networks still remain.

This period changed things for many people: the meaning of politics (I can be part of politics without being an actual politician); the awareness of being a political subject; and the attitude towards municipal administration (I should have a say on the projects being implemented in my neighborhood). During this period, there was a decrease in the daily use of parks and public spaces, followed by an increase in the legitimacy of small platforms, initiatives, and solidarities.

Is shared space necessarily communal or are we in need of new terms to describe experiences of collectively shaped and maintained shared space (e.g. common space, liberated space, self-managed space, autonomous space etc.)
I don't think every shared space is communal. I think each example is case-specific.

A self-managed space could be communal or highly commercial. A liberated space can become a space highly controlled by a single group etc. A shared space which is also self-managed and horizontally organized is:
   a. a means for testing the relations and the kind of life that we imagine;
   b. a bringing together of people that helps create a common platform inside a system which tries to separate us from each other and encourages only competition;
   c. an open space of possibilities because the coming together and the sharing of experiences often produces unexpected results.

If "commoning" is a term to describe practices of sharing which directly affect social relations and shape social bonds, do you think that certain aspects of your collective experiences may be described as commoning? What are the most important areas of sharing in a society according to your view?
Combining with the question: What is the role of urban movements in shaping alternative views about city and society?
During the Gezi Resistance, the importance of the issues which were highlighted by the politics of "commoning" was proven once again. AKP's neoliberal policy, which is based on the

"renting" of the city, does not take any opposition into account, ignoring the demands of the masses. Furthermore, it has covered most available green space with concrete, pushed the urban poor away from the city center, and transformed the city center into dead spaces designated only for touristic use. These policies, the Taksim pedestrianization project, and finally the planned shopping mall in Gezi Park caused a high level of public reaction. The importance of urban struggle, local resistance, and their mobilizing effect, which until the Gezi Resistance had been at the bottom of the list of the central campaigns of the traditional left, have become accepted by the masses.

The most important tactic to be developed against the government, which had established a strategy to isolate us and minimize our contact with each other, was solidarity, the experience of forming shared lives in spaces that we claimed as ours. During the communal life formed in Gezi Park, this possibility was tested for the first time on a large scale.

Against the policies of the government, which drew boundaries and seized our places, the dispersed counter-enclosure actions were forced to recede until the day when the struggle turned into a large-scale resistance by the participation of the masses. Although defense line first aimed to protect existing urban common resources, within the organization of life in Gezi Park, in the long run, rather than being a defense line, it started to create future wishes and new forms of relations and spaces concerning us all. In this way, it played a key role in changing the feeling of fragmentation and powerlessness and in re-establishing the "public." I think this is also why the government's reaction increased in time.

Architecture and alternative urban futures

What was the role of engaged specialists (architects, urban planners, lawyers, economists, etc.) in practices of space-production connected to the Gezi occupation experience?
The Chamber of Architects: they were following the case of the Taksim pedestrianization project from the beginning. They played a crucial role in challenging the legality of the administra-

tion's decisions and by explaining the project's problems to the public and thus raising public awareness.

Syndicates: in the first days of the protests they supplied the logistics, tents and blankets, food and sound systems.

Independent architects and urban planners: some of them created an archive of self-built structures in the park, and made drawings of them. Some city planners prepared and updated the map of the organizations in the park.

Volunteer lawyers: they followed arrests and detentions. They helped thousands of people.

Health professionals: they organized and maintained many emergency healthcare tents and helped wounded people voluntarily.

People with media experience, artists, journalists etc.: they helped in forming radio stations, fanzines, web pages for counter-information, and kept a wide archive of images, videos, and articles.

What is a city for you? How would you define an ideal city? Can there be forms of social organization that will make contemporary metropolises places of sharing and equality? Can such forms give new meaning to everyday habits and everyday problems of survival?

I think an ideal city depends on many things, such as its size, the geography it is in, the history of the city etc. I don't have a prepared answer for that.

But I know what I want from a city because I live in one. I want it to be more accessible for everyone; I don't want its public spaces to become privatized; I don't want its memorial spaces and green areas to disappear. I want an ecological city; I want equal participation for everyone in the decision-making processes; I want better public transportation and less cars, cheaper transportation for 24 hours.

And as a woman I want a woman- and queer-friendly city. I want to feel safe in the city any hour, in any street and with whatever clothes I wear. And I don't want this safety coming from the police but out of bonds of mutual understanding and solidarity.

Can you see in your experiences and struggles elements of a future, more just, society? Do your acts "prefigure," in a way, the future society you long for? Is there a legacy of the Gezi Park occupation that connects to current struggles in Turkey?

I might be a little optimist but yes I do see the past experiences already changing things. And not only local struggles but also we are learning from struggles of other localities. I think we should think in longer terms. It has been only 3 years after Gezi and especially after the recent coup d'état we are passing through the roughest of times. Yet even the smallest changes have potential for the future.

None of the traditional left parties was able to continue the same way. They had to adapt themselves to a new political language or get divided and disappear.

All over the city, parks were claimed by the people and they are being used more than before.

Many young people were politicized during the Gezi occupation, and for them being engaged with politics will mean something different from what our generation thought about it.

Some municipalities opened up their doors to local actors and it will be hard to step back from this participatory form.

Many smaller movements had the chance to introduce their struggles to others and some permanent and temporary alliances were set.

Many rural struggles found more support from the cities.

And I think, more importantly, even after so much violence and even though some Southeast Turkish cities were being bombed for days, and people were being fired from their jobs for political reasons, I can't still see any political apathy. People might be afraid to be on the streets but they are not disconnected with politics. We just need a break and a space to breathe, to come out from our corners.

5

Commoning neighborhoods: resisting urban renewal in Barcelona's periphery

In search for the potentialities of emancipatory commoning, a lot is to be learned by studying practices of cohabitation in housing complexes. We know that in most cases people are forced to live together under conditions that they never chose merely because they don't have other options. Neighborhoods of so-called affordable housing programs or social housing complexes more often than not become stigmatized areas for the urban poor. Mass housing projects generally produce anonymity and alienation and discourage collective initiatives that would form a shared feeling of belonging to a neighborhood community.

Housing, however, can be treated as a problem closely connected to the social perspective of commoning. Instead of approaching housing complexes as a more or less standardized set of private houses, it is possible to analyze and envisage them as potential areas of urban commoning, in which shared uses and practices of collaboration prevail. Such an approach would critically reformulate housing as a problem and would enrich the search for inhabitation practices that are shaped by sharing.

In the three chapters that follow, three different relevant research areas are explored in an indicative way. The first has to do with the potentialities of common life that develop in a state-produced social housing complex almost in spite of its design and largely due to its specific history. The second focuses on social housing complexes produced through participatory design and production practices that inventively activated existing urban

commoning traditions. And the third explores advanced potentialities of emancipatory commoning that were created in self-
managed autonomous neighborhoods produced by politically
engaged social movements.

All three chapters are more than case studies. In each of them,
theory issues connected to the prospect of reformulating the
problem of cohabitation in the context of this book's argument
about emancipatory commoning are discussed. From the first
to the third of these chapters there emerges a kind of progressive proliferation of emancipatory potentialities: from the ad
hoc struggles to preserve a rich tradition of common life in the
Bon Pastor neighborhood, to the Brazilian mutual help homeless
movement projects crucially aided by the USINA architectural
group, and then to Mexican autonomous designed neighborhoods, there seems to be a kind gradual approach to the scope of
emancipated society. However, possibilities for further advances
towards this scope exist in all three cases and in the different types
of house commoning they represent. To be able to talk about
those possibilities, one has to analyze even more deeply the socio-
historical context of their present status. And this, of course, is
beyond the scope of this book.

Re-inventing social housing?

Lots of people today live in social housing complexes which are
in urgent need of re-design and maintenance while being under
threat of demolition due to predatory "urban renewal" projects.
How can a politically engaged architecture help those people
develop and maintain their common life against market forces
and privatization policies? How can inhabitants' struggles as well
as their everyday inventiveness generate proposals that protect
and encourage alternative values of cohabitation based on urban
commoning?

We live in a period of devastating austerity policies and relentless neoliberal attacks on the public sector. Social housing used
to be an emblematic welfare activity of the pre-neoliberal state.
But it was also the result of continuous struggles and organized
demands connected to the rights of those who cannot afford their

shelter in the city. Today, in most countries, social housing has lost its social meaning and has been integrated in various ways to the real estate market (Schwartz 2006, Scanlon and Whitehead 2008, Minton 2009). However, fewer people than ever today to have access to an affordable appropriate dwelling. Re-inventing social housing is an urgent political act and an urgent alternative design task. Re-defining common spaces of cohabitation and practices of communal living may become crucially important in a period during which public space is aggressively privatized and shared spaces are becoming extinct.

This chapter focuses on the history and current potentialities of a social housing complex in Barcelona, which may be considered both as emblematic and exceptional: emblematic because in its history and threatened everydayness it epitomizes the commoning spirit that prevails in such urban communities; exceptional because it has not only become the site of important struggles connected to shared values and aspirations based on community experiences but also the focus of an international architectural competition meant to explore alternatives to "urban renewal."

The case of the Bon Pastor social housing complex in Barcelona gives us the opportunity to explore the dynamics of the social housing type of cohabitation by interpreting both the forms of struggle through commoning (and commoning through struggle) and the potential spaces of commoning which could be envisaged through socially aware architectural design. For this scope, the chapter includes the presentation of a proposal that was submitted to the competition *Repensar Bon Pastor* (a proposal made by M. Kopanari, S. Sophianopoulos, F. Vatavali, and S. Stavrides). An interview with one of the activists of Bon Pastor who was also central to the organizing of the competition will present the rich potential and impasses of this struggle to preserve and develop an exemplary case of urban commoning.

The Bon Pastor competition managed to combine two important perspectives in social and architectural research. The one is firmly focused on urgent social needs and tries to explore ways through which those needs can be detected, expanded, and possibly satisfied in urban everydayness. The other draws on the exploration of shared dreams for a different future and attempts to discover ways to study those collective aspirations and to give them shape in space. Both perspectives converged in the context of this competition on the housing problem and the search for possible exemplary or experimental solutions.

The Bon Pastor social housing complex used to be (and still is) an area with a rich communal and public life. The space of the neighborhood reflects the complexity and inventiveness that characterizes the habits of its inhabitants. And it was because of these collective habits that people struggled to defend their neighborhood from plans of "urban renewal" and "urban development" (well-known euphemisms for real estate profit making).

The Bon Pastor competition was a means to support inhabitants' struggle but also a way to explore communal values of cohabitation. People tend to collectively invent forms of shared life, especially in housing areas in which everyday commoning habits prevail. They tend to organize their private and common life by projecting shared values onto the built environment. Just a walk around the neighborhood, especially before the demolition

5.1 In the streets of Bon Pastor

of many of the houses, was enough for someone to be impressed by the variety of self-built house extensions, the diversity of private yard uses, the rich street life, and the multiple methods of communication between the neighbors. Even the local habits of bird singing contests and dove races contribute to the weaving of communal bonds which are expressed in every mundane everyday activity.

Learning form Greek social housing communities

Cohabitation practices in the context of social housing complexes differ according to socio-historical contingencies. And of course a crucial distinguishing factor has to do with the scale of the corresponding projects and their level of integration into the city which they become part of. Bon Pastor neighborhood is far away from the Barcelona city center and at the time of the competition it was a characteristic low density, low class housing area. Communal bonds were developed between the inhabitants and a dense network of everyday exchanges was still active.

A comparison with social housing communities which developed in relevant complexes in Athens could be instructive because, in spite of differences in the social housing policy traditions (and in the actual socio-economic conditions which made those policies possible), a certain culture-based commoning ethos left its mark in complexes similar in scale to Bon Pastor. In search for those marks, which are active in the collective memory of the inhabitants, this part of the chapter will invite aspects of the Athenian social housing history into the discussion about Bon Pastor's future. Moreover, it was the participation in the Bon Pastor competition that inspired members of the aforementioned team to embark on a research project focused on the transformations of public space in Greek social housing complexes. Thus, some of the research findings of this project, which document the rich traditions of space commoning in Athens social housing complexes, will be called upon in order to substantiate the potentialities of shared life which a proposal for the Bon Pastor competition tried to develop. To put it another way, the experience of this research made some of us retrospectively understand what kind of life we were trying to promote and sustain through our architectural proposal.

Especially influenced by the mid-war architectural discussion on minimum dwelling (Heynen 1999: 43–50), the architects of the 1930s social housing buildings focused their efforts on devising an ideal small apartment type to be produced in large quantities. As one can easily observe, this apartment type was similar to those used in many cases throughout Europe for similar buildings, albeit in considerably larger quantities. The idea was to provide shelter for the poor working-class families by explicitly enhancing family values and the "autonomy" of a nuclear sociality. Thus, shared spaces were mainly only approached as necessary organizational areas which would accommodate circulation and direct access to private apartments rather than as encounter places which would enhance sociality and collectivity. Staircases were, in most cases, merely staircase-wells for vertical movement. And outdoor spaces were in many cases left un- or under-designed, thus often becoming a no-man's land.

An important change may be observed in the 1950s' and 1960s' social housing design approaches in Greece. The Workers Housing Organization (OEK) was formed in 1955 and marks a period in which a kind of welfare state was being established in the country. OEK was not exactly a state controlled organization. The OEK board included representatives of the Confederation of Workers Union and the Greek Industrialists Association as well as appointed officials of the Ministry of Work. Although it was founded on the premise of being funded by the public sector in combination with obligatory contributions of employers and employees, OEK ended being totally dependent on the contributions. Workers representatives were actually not involved at all in the establishing of design principles for the housing areas according to projected needs that might describe working-class ethics or aspirations. The idea of typological choices, standardization, and large-scale uniformity seem never to have been questioned. Of course, during the after-war years, the family apartment in a relatively low rise multistory building emblematized for the working classes the promise of social ascent (Leontidou 1990). Choices made by the OEK architects and planners were more or less in compliance with dominating individualist ideologies prevailing on the working classes too.

Designing urban neighborhoods from scratch has not only been a modernist dream (Le Corbusier 1987, Kwinter 2002) but a concrete challenge in recent history, especially after the Second World War in Europe. In Greece this challenge was rather met with mere pragmatism than with the idealist projections which influenced visionary architects of the German Weimar Republic, the Red Vienna administration, or the early Soviet experimental programs of mass housing. Pragmatism obviously tends to focus on quantifiable needs than on experiments in new spatialities and social relationships. Whereas new urban areas were envisaged by the socially engaged architects of the 1920s and 1930s as opportunities to design for a future "better" society, in Greece the architects of OEK or of the so-called Welfare Ministry more or less took for granted that social housing neighborhoods would develop along dominating individualistic values. Public space or communal space design was, thus, either largely neglected or formed according to the predominance of the nuclear family's closed universe. The opportunity to experiment with new kinds of shared spaces was lost although the modernist planning principles (including the free floating block) asked for a rethinking of open space and public space.

It was the residents of those complexes who in many cases converted anonymous spaces in-between the buildings to communal spaces. Strangely this was often established through practices of appropriation of circulation spaces. For example, in building complexes in which access to individual apartments was through open air elevated corridors, people used the space in front of their apartment's entrance as an ad hoc shared balcony. Meeting neighbors as they were crossing those balconies to reach their own apartments added opportunities of everyday negotiations and created experiences of space-sharing. It was, of course, up to those specific developing relationships to convert or develop such opportunities to practices of space commoning. Architectural form, however, in those cases supported the potentiality of common space.

Another area for communal life improvisations was the terrace.

Vassilis, a resident of social housing at Rentis neighborhood (in his sizties when the interview was conducted) remembers: "We often used to gather in one apartment to enjoy a shared meal and some wine. We also used the terrace when the weather was fine. There was a common barbecue, some chairs, a small table … From the terrace we all launched our kites on Ash Monday [note: a tradition still very much alive in Greece]. You could not see the sky! And radios were playing … When I was a young boy I used to improvise shadow theater puppet performances on the terrace for my friends to watch. Most housewives met on the terrace to wash the family's clothes. We used to play between the linen that was put out to dry" (Stavrides et al. 2009).

This is just one among many narrated reminiscences that describe experiences of space commoning. Terraces of three-to-four-story buildings were indeed common spaces to be used mainly by the corresponding building's inhabitants. Laundry installations in those terraces became meeting points for the women. Let us not forget that the early 1930s, as well as the early 1960s (to which Vassilis explicitly refers), were periods in which family ties, as well as a clear division of labor between the sexes, were really strong, especially in working-class neighborhoods. We need not romanticize these collective practices then: a lot of strict social role prescriptions were active. Hierarchies were either latent or explicit depending on the history of each family. Inculcated codes of behavior indeed created geometries of power inside the family, although families considered as units of the neighborhood community were more or less equal between them in terms of rights and obligations. Commoning, thus, unfolded explicitly between families and was based on a community of inhabitants which was either founded on shared descent and history (as in the case of refugee social housing settlements) or on a feeling of belonging to the same class and sharing the same everyday habits (in the case of OEK complexes).

It is interesting to compare those collective experiences of common space production and use with some similar ones that are developing today in Athens in a different socio-historical context but in the same buildings. At the Petrina (Rentis) complex, apartments are mostly being rented nowadays by Pakistani immigrants: "In about 15 houses here live Pakistani people. In each apartment stay 2–5 persons. We all know each other because we came from the same village, Malikonal" (Stavrides et al. 2009). Those people too have developed their own version of space commoning. Compared to the Greek residents, their attitude towards public space is more cautious and perhaps even restrained. They feel that their stay in Greece is temporary. Their house and family (Pakistani immigrants are usually only men) are far away and wait for them. So they mostly organize their shared space inside courtyards or on apartment balconies. Mundane everyday practices, as well as ceremonially exceptional ones (such as having a haircut on the day of a religious feast), punctuate the rhythms of those practices as they unfold in the creation of shared spaces.

Architectural design choices seem to help in certain ways in the development of space commoning. Low-profile collective appropriations of outdoor spaces by Pakistani tenants becomes possible because most of such spaces are not totally exposed to public view. Entrances to buildings reveal only partly what goes on in the small courtyards or on the first-floor shared balconies. Various kinds of boundaries constructed by the ground floor apartment owners also help Pakistani renters to organize a carefully "protected" common life. Their community depends, of course, on shared habits and class characteristics (almost all work in the nearby central vegetable market) but is strongly based on a shared longing for a homeland which is far away.

As in the case of the Bon Pastor buildings, the design of social housing complexes in Athens was based on the idea of developing individual house models which were to be produced in quantities and in uniform patterns. The nuclear family (along with the social ordering resulting from it being considered as the unit out of which society should be organized) was at the center of this design approach, often with less concern about community spaces or public spaces. It was the inhabitants' direct involvement that actually transformed existing public spaces to shared spaces. As explicitly presented in Stefano Portelli's interview (which follows) and as documented in the research project referred to, inhabitants managed to develop spaces of commoning often in spite of design choices that promoted functional anonymity (in the streets of Bon Pastor and in the terraces of Athenian complexes). In certain cases, as in the Pakistani tenants' use of protected shared courtyards and pavement areas, and in the uses of small "private" yards of Bon Pastor (all defined by osmotic boundaries), interesting experiences of in-between spaces develop. Space commoning, thus, does not flourish in areas in which shared or public ownership of space is explicitly defined, but overspills such legal boundaries. Exchanges and negotiations that establish collectively agreed upon habits as well as everyday encounters weave a colorful social fabric which potentializes space through sharing.

Space commoning as a challenge to uniformity

When we visited Bon Pastor as a team of architects-researchers seeking to learn more about this neighborhood in order to participate in the competition, we found that beyond an apparent uniformity in building types and layout the area was characterized by a rich diversification of individual houses which evolved through the inhabitant's active involvement. Our observations, directly focused on the socio-spatial context of a rich communal life were these:

a. A developed network of communicating households helps inhabitants orient themselves in a recognizable community.
b. A common cultural background is expressed in ways of using public space as well as in ways of enjoying after work leisure opportunities. People tend to find their own reference points in the neighborhood and to share some particular forms of collective play as in the characteristic "bird contests" for which many hours of preparation are necessary.
c. However, there are differences in collective habits connected with some particular forms of family structure. Roma people, who were relocated in the area, carry different traditions and emphatically express them in various forms of public space appropriation.
d. Different ways of life develop in almost full view of each other, exactly because those differences are allowed to negotiate in public space. Particular social characteristics and

different social identities are expressed in public and are not
secluded in closed private shelters. Life in the streets offers
to those identities a rich negotiating ground.

e. From the ways house facades are purposely and inventively
differentiated we can infer a decisive factor of identity
negotiations. People differentiate their houses by creating
marks of family collective identities only because they share
common, recognizable codes.

f. Collective memory recognizes in the image of the neighborhood space, which has remained almost unchanged
throughout the years, the emblematic representation of a
shared life. For the inhabitants the neighborhood constitutes a world marked by history, a world full of recognizable
traces.

The specific urban configuration of the studied neighborhood supports this social life in important ways. Private houses communicate directly between themselves and with the streets. Although the
general layout seems to produce the image of a military camp, the
essential differentiation of the main axes creates a characteristic
identifiable structure. Public space, thus, is potentially organized
in squares, main routes, and secondary streets.

Standardized layout does not simply produce similar and anonymous spaces, although mass production housing is connected
with such results. The specific layout gives form and orientation
to the neighborhood and can establish an easily graspable urban
identity. Open and straight streets provide the ground for ephemeral appropriations of public space by keeping the corresponding
spatial practices exposed to each other. The street network thus
contributes to the experience of shared public space.

Because of pressing everyday needs, inhabitants have built additional rooms in the courtyards. However, as the plans and images
of all of the 1929 *Casas Baratas* projects show, those courtyards
contained crucial parts of a common everyday life (comparable
as they are with corresponding structures in the Barcelona shanty
towns of the 1920s).

It was this spirit of producing diversity out of uniformity
without losing sight of a shared urban identity that we tried to

incorporate in our proposal. There seems to be a major challenge for contemporary design nowadays which is connected both to urgent needs and to important aspirations: how to re-invent social housing? And connected to this major challenge is the foundational challenge underlying social housing production: can we integrate a design and production process based on the cheap construction of large numbers of housing units with the search for individuality inside a community, the search for particularity and differentiation inside shared worlds?

Mass housing?

Mass housing production process, and the idea of "people" as a description of a unified body of society members, seem to be mutually compatible in representations of modern society, in which homogenization and mass production prevail. Modernist proposals explicitly targeted the creation of a generic figure: the "new man," the "modern man," considered as a figure with standard needs and therefore as a figure destined to live in standardized urban environments. Uniformity was not an accident in modernist planning.

   Facing the problem of uniformity or, rather, facing uniformity in social housing architecture as a problem, entails a rethink, not only of modernist principles and aspirations but also of society in its contemporary form. If it is true that diversification or multiplicity characterizes forms of life in contemporary societies, then it is necessary to understand what the needs and value choices are that either praise this multiplicity or condemn it. In short, if we face the architectural challenge of introducing to urban environments in which uniformity prevails (and most social housing complexes are such environments), forms that differentiate, then what should these forms positively or negatively express? And if we are in search of expressing and enhancing urban commons (and urban commoning), what role could we attribute to form differentiation? Is the contemporary commoning culture one focused on the discovery of a new Whole, a new One (and thus of a new Unity based on repetition and similarity) or a culture focused on the confluence of differences, on the creation of shared common worlds which, nevertheless, sustain and promote (rather than tolerate) diversity?

The theories connected to the emergence of the multitude considered as the characteristic body to today's society explicitly problematize the relation between multiplicity and communality, between common abilities and resources and individual (even singular) practices that support diverse forms of social existence. As Hardt and Negri summarize: "The multitude is a diffuse set of singularities that produce a common life … The common which is at once an artificial result and constitutive basis, is what configures the mobile and flexible substance of the multitude" (2005: 349).

If modernist mass housing was designed for the people, can today's interventions attempt to express the needs of the multitudes? Responses to this question may indeed return to the problem of typology.

In his critique of an emblematic, as well as controversial, mass housing building, the Byker Wall, Alan Colquhoun summarizes the problem of typology in contemporary housing architecture: "what sets out to provide an equivalent of the traditional ensemble, in which the basic set is culturally determined and individual choice is restricted to matters of detail, is, in fact, an entirely individual concept. As such it belongs to the tradition of 'total design'" (1985: 102). Architectural design (or architectural interventions in existing housing buildings) has to face the following dilemma: it will have to propose solutions to the mass housing problem based on either the multiplication of diversifying architectural elements in order to avoid the condemned uniform environments of rigid typologies, or the randomness produced by inhabitants' interventions which will, nevertheless, be made possible (or even encouraged) by ingenuous infrastructure design (unavoidably also based on a typology-oriented design process). The second choice differs from the first one regarding the role assigned to typological reasoning (thinking through typology): while the first choice sees typology as an established canvas for designed and constructed variations, the second one attempts to predict possible needs through typology, establishing, thus, a more or less wide field of possibilities. From typology as a set of rules defining existing spaces to typology as a set of potentialities defining possible spaces.

Responses to the social housing design problems may attempt to discover the architectural equivalents of "individuation processes," considered as processes that actually stem from pre-existing shared worlds. As Virno insists: "For the people universality is a *promise*, for the many it is a *premise* ... The multitude is backed up by the One of language, by the intellect as public or inter-psychological resource, and the generic faculties of the species" (Virno 2015b: 222; emphasis in original). Transferred to the problem of individuation in and through space, this logic may take the shared urban world as a premise (created by the generic tendency to identify a community with a "place") and explore diversity as a necessary path towards singular spaces for singular lives. And because individuation as a process that creates singularities can only be understood as something that needs to develop in the different temporalities of shared worlds, an appropriate choice of design might be to provide future inhabitants with the means to shape their space starting from what they share with others. Individuation, as Virno, using Simondon, tells us, is never complete (Virno 2015b: 234–236). That is why perhaps it is a potentially creative process as long as it never denies its foundation on commonality, on what is common. Reinventing differentiation in and through space is not necessarily a postmodernist glorification of uniqueness (with the corresponding glorification of buildings as unique "objects" and architects as "unique" creators) but it may be an exercise of commoning in architecture that is based on the rise of the culture of the multitude. Using this as a criterion we can distinguish design proposals which attempt to support and express a social housing community's shared world while establishing in this world and through it individualized spaces (for individuals, families, or small inhabitant groups), from design proposals which merely celebrate diversification while ignoring the corresponding community's common life patterns.

A proposal

The competition *Repensar Bon Pastor* was launched in response to an aggressive urban renewal project adopted by the *Patronat* of Barcelona in 2003. By 2007, 145 houses had already been demol-

5.2 Destroying a rich commoning neighborhood tradition (Bon Pastor, Barcelona)

ished in the first phase of the project, and in many cases people were violently evicted (Col.Lectiu Repensar Bonpastor 2016).

The logic of the project is based on a neoliberal reasoning which considers the Bon Pastor houses as "obsolete" (Col.Lectiu Repensar Bonpastor 2016) and aims at giving the residents the opportunity to become homeowners of small buildings. The "cleared" land resulting from the demolitions and the replacement of existing one-story houses with multistory housing buildings (which would be "affordable" housing rather than social housing) is to be used, according to the project, for land speculation (houses and shops for sale).

For some of the tenants (the old houses are owned by Barcelona's City Council) the promise of homeownership seemed alluring. However, those who followed the proposal scheme (willingly or not) soon discovered that the loans they had to get in order to pay for their houses were becoming an unbearable burden (added to housing taxation obligations), which was way more difficult to carry than the rents they had to pay before.

Responding to the competition's call for the proposal of "new alternatives for Bon Pastor's transformation" we indeed tried as a group of architects to suggest ways to rehabilitate the *casas baratas* without ignoring the "architectural, historical and ethnological value of this housing typology" (Col.Lectiu Repensar Bonpastor 2016, 7–11). Thus, as a first move, we actually proposed the redrawing of the housing block limits in the area. The "new housing block" considered as a "new urban unit" will consist of two neighboring blocks and the street that used to separate them. The resulting block will contain a common space to be used by the block's inhabitants as shared outdoor space and as a common courtyard which will be connected to the network of surrounding streets and to the neighborhood's small squares. Through this design strategy, diverse spaces of common use are to be created, in which small groups of inhabitants may organize

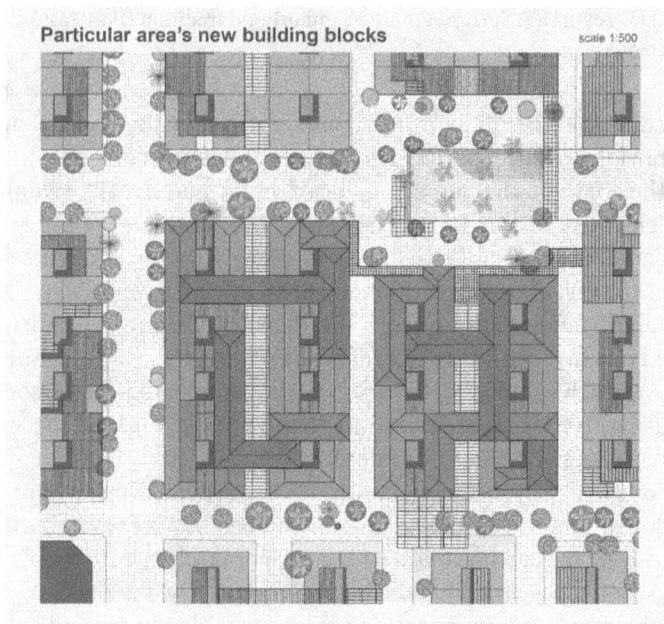

5.3 A proposal for Bon Pastor: respecting urban layout while introducing an additional floor

a shared everydayness. Open spaces will thus constitute a network of interconnected urban thresholds which will create permeable boundaries between different spaces of shared use.

This strategy is focused on the support of existing commoning practices and tries, through choices that target urban form (spatial form-as-organization), to create opportunities for the Bon Pastor community to preserve and expand its space sharing traditions. At the same time, this proposal makes it possible to construct additional stories to the existing one-story buildings (up to three as a maximum) in ways that will integrate the new apartments into a rich network of shared spaces within each new block. Proposing that some apartments bridge the block's in-between streets this project introduces outdoor spaces on different levels and actually recreates and extends the network of threshold-like common spaces which mediate between the city public space and the private family space. In addition to this, some of the already abandoned or "closed" houses can be re-designed as small communal spaces or small shops in support of the neighborhood's everyday life.

It would obviously be a gesture of bypassing the social housing problem to propose a remodeling of the houses by keeping the

A «new building block» located on one of the two proposed main squares

5.4 A proposal for Bon Pastor: a more densely populated neighborhood does not have to be created by alienating high-rise buildings

same density. To propose a density characteristic of suburban conditions in an area that is meant to be kept as a social housing area would be unrealistic. A moderate rise in density, however, will ensure that this proposal will offer a convincing alternative to the urban renewal plans without succumbing to the pressure of neoliberal development mythology.

Furthermore, the proposed typology of apartments is based on the existing house types without the overall arrangement remain-

Figure 1: View of the block's semi-covered inner street

Figure 2: View of a block's corner on the main pedestrian axis

5.5 A proposal for Bon Pastor: redesigning public space by introducing common space potentialities

ing attached to the initial scheme's monotonous uniformity. Learning from the ways inhabitants have inventively modified the houses with ad-hoc extensions and additions of outdoor space, this proposal aims to encourage and activate the direct involvement of the neighborhood's inhabitants themselves. Assemblies and established negotiation traditions may very well integrate collectively agreed upon interventions to a flexible overall plan. Returning to the problem of uniformity versus singularity, and to the opposition between commoning and individualism, this proposal may indeed give people the means to preserve the characteristic cultural pluralism of the neighborhood within the shared ethos of belonging which has, throughout Bon Pastor's history, sustained a rich communal life.

Interview with Stefano Portelli, anthropologist and member of the Col.Lectiu Repensar Bonpastor, 30 October 2016

Public space, common space

How is public space produced in your settlement (or neighborhood)? Who decides – what are the practices of such space production?
Bon Pastor was founded in the 1920s as one of a series of planned settlements in which to displace migrant workers from the center of Barcelona. Its 784 houses were too small to host the extended families that shared the rent, and since the very beginning of its existence, streets and plazas served as an extension of the private space. In the streets, negotiations took place over cohabitation; the informal norms to live together were produced; and conflicts were solved and relations established. Those who played as children in the street later lived together through adulthood and old age: the street came to symbolize the relationship among people over time. This centrality of the street was celebrated in periodic rituals, like the big open air meals among neighbors, or the annual feast of Saint Joan, with its ritual bonfires and rumba music and dance, with which neighbors periodically wiped out the conflicts that developed between them. We could say that the streets in Bon Pastor are a metaphor for the community; so the fondness that residents have of "their" public space is a physical transposition of the affection and bonds that link them with each other. All of this started to change with the demolitions; by destroying the houses and the streets that separated them, the City Council also dismantled all this structure that ensured the collective production

of space and of society, a structure that was invisible, but of crucial importance to the community.

Is it important to develop different forms of public space?
Even if structurally all the streets of Bon Pastor had the same physical form – the urbanistic structure of the neighborhood is a uniform and repetitive grid – each street was lived and even physically modified according to the needs and desires of those who lived in it. So the neighborhood presented an impressive array of internal differences: there were streets that were quiet and clean, others that were messy and full of naughty kids annoying residents and visitors alike. There were plazas where some felt at ease, like the older residents or the first settlers, and other squares where other residents felt comfortable, like the newly arrived Roma and former slum dwellers relocated in the 1980s and 1990s. But permeability among these different spaces, and, thus, links between the different communities that inhabited them, was one of the main features of the neighborhood, something the residents were aware of and proud of. In the new spatial order after the demolitions – vertical blocks – it is much more difficult to find spaces of negotiation and communication among the different groups; so there is a stronger tendency towards internal segregation and ghettoization.

Do you see any difference between public and communal space?
Formally, all Bon Pastor is "public." Its lands and the houses built upon them legally belong to the City Council, their construction was financed with public money, and the residents only pay the rent. But in practice, the neighborhood had been neglected by the public authorities who were in charge, and the neighbors were forced to take care of the space, both public and private. This self-organization was mostly illegal, since formally it was the City Council who had to refurbish and maintain the houses; since it didn't, the residents felt legitimated to do it by themselves. This is how the space became "common," from public that it was. Most work was done in common, so the spaces produced were felt as somewhat "belonging" to those who invested their work and money in refurbishing them. The City Council was felt as

having less and less right to claim its property, though it formally remained the legal owner. From the point of view of urban studies, the neighborhood should not be considered as "public," since its residents don't feel that public authorities are entitled to make decisions about its future. People consider the neighborhood as their collective possession, and interpret the initiatives of the City Council over their space as an abuse. Obviously they frame this belief in different terms than those that scholars or political activists will use.

Please refer to some crucial events that shaped this settlement and its forms of organization.
I believe that most of the autonomous forms of use of the space that can still be found in Bon Pastor could be traced back to the extraordinary time of workers' emancipation that immediately followed the foundation of the neighborhood. Immediately after Bon Pastor was built, a great social turmoil began, that led first to the social Revolution of 1931, then to the declaration of the Spanish Republic in 1936, finally to the Spanish Civil War. Bon Pastor was one of the leading neighborhoods in the widespread culture of workers' emancipation and autonomy that Franco's regime had brutally repressed since 1939. From the neighborhood, hundreds of volunteers joined the militias that fought fascism in Aragó and on the river Ebro, where many died; it was specifically targeted by the reactionary forces, with bombing and later with reprisals, for being a hotspot of unruliness and revolutionary working-class culture. The memory of these events can still be found in Bon Pastor's streets, but more as a widespread mistrust and disobedience to power, than as a formalized memory of historical events

Please describe the ways of decision-making in terms of the settlement's layout, the rules of building and the regulations of the settlement's maintenance.
There is currently no formalized "horizontal" decision-making process among residents, since most decisions are taken by a neighbors' association (the Asociación de Vecinos), which was long ago co-opted by the political parties. It was born as an

expression of collective power during the dictatorship, but today is little more than the spokesperson of the City Council in the neighborhood. Alternative associations were born to claim the right of residents to represent themselves, one of which is the Associació Avis del Barri, which promoted the collective research project I was involved in. But now internal divisions among these groups undermine the possibility for collective decision-making processes; this is a direct consequence of the urban renewal process that the City Council implemented in the neighborhood.

What does it mean for you to share space? What is the meaning of private space for you?
When I lived in the houses of Bon Pastor, before the demolition, I appreciated very much the sense of openness that private space had, the permeability of houses to the street. Neighbors passed by and sometimes knocked, children could play in the plaza in front of the house – we could watch them while doing our work at home. Though this sometimes meant a lack of privacy, which some residents resent, it certainly meant less loneliness for the elderly, more help for mothers with many children, and a general awareness of each other. Even if there were conflicts, everybody knew that the neighborhood kept an eye on them, and if this was uncomfortable when it turned to gossip, it was an enviable resource in case of trouble. In my opinion, even those who claimed their need to more private space miss these intrusions in their privacy, now that they are lost. The new blocks were presented by the City Council as finally providing people with the privacy that the houses couldn't guarantee; but vulnerable people need privacy less than they need mutual help and collective care of each other. Especially in times of crisis, when all that is not private is needed much more by the most vulnerable people, to highlight just the need for private space is an excuse to justify the dispossession of public or common spaces.

Community

How does your community organize itself? Are we talking about a stable community, an expanding community?
The community of Bon Pastor's residents has been disbanded as a consequence of an urban renewal process. Most people are still in the area, but internal relationships and forms of organizing deeply changed as the space was transformed, and as the residents were relocated into newly built flats. The trauma of relocation and demolition could perhaps be overcome in some years, or decades, but the community that once was, with its strength and weaknesses, surely is no longer.

What are the relations of the Bon Pastor community to its members' past? Did they belong to rural communities or to different urban communities?
Most residents of Bon Pastor come from the great wave of migration from Southern Spain that entered Barcelona at the beginning of the twentieth century. Waged workers and day laborers of Murcia and Andalusia were considered undesirable citizens by the authorities, and were either cleared from the slums they inhabited or deported from the city center towards peripheral neighborhoods like Bon Pastor. In the following decades, the neighborhood received outcasts, victims of the most varied stories of exclusion and displacement, but mostly coming from other urban communities that had been disbanded or gentrified. So residents of Bon Pastor are long-term Barcelonian citizens, coming mainly from the more vulnerable city sectors, and although they have contributed to the growth of the city, they are treated as marginal.

Please describe the ways you have approached as a community the problem of social inequality. Do you think that inequality is being shaped differently in cities than in rural areas? Is there any meaning for you in the term "spatial justice"?
Inequality in Bon Pastor takes many different forms. It takes the form of gender violence, which often goes unpunished by the state authorities, and which is accepted as normal by a huge sector of the population. It takes the form of drug and alcohol abuse,

which for many is the only escape from the burdens imposed by an economic system that structurally needs them unemployed. It takes the form of spatial segregation, which prevents easy access to the rest of Barcelona, turning the neighborhood into a ghetto for some, especially the young. To these and other constraints, residents used to have collective answers, for instance in the 1960s and 1970s when neighbors' associations provided care and gave voice to many harsh situations of injustice. But since then, many of these structures of mutual help have been replaced with state institutions, as social services or public healthcare; even if these structures manage funds through which many situations can be addressed, often they are trapped into prejudices that end up reproducing or even contributing to the situation of injustice.

Did you collectively draw examples for self-management from shared traditions? Is collective memory a source for social experiments of collaboration? In what way?
I mentioned the heritage of the social revolution of the 1930s as a powerful reference for self-management and self-help. Although it might not be explicit for many residents, mostly uneducated, there is a shared memory of being excluded and resisting segregation, which shapes the collective identity and practices of the neighborhood. Collaboration in such a thick and dense urban fabric is felt as the essence of living there. Even if always in controversial and conflictive forms, the strategies of cohabitation that residents developed over time represent an experiment of an alternative urban way of living, which should be considered as a source of inspiration for other, more publicly respected, sectors of the city.

Sharing and commoning

Do you think it is important to develop practices of sharing? How?
In a situation like the one that the residents of Bon Pastor are experiencing, especially after the crisis of 2007, sharing resources is not only an issue of being nice to each other. It is a vital need for those who can't claim possession of anything individually. Residents of Bon Pastor don't own their houses; those who tried

to buy the flats often found themselves trapped into the criminal requirements of banks, backed by the state, which plunge them into debt and sometimes result in evictions. Those who own nothing can only rely on what is common, in order to ensure sheer survival. But the insistence of public policies on private property, on bank mortgages, and on individual solutions to collective problems, clashes with both the culture and the economic possibilities of the people they address.

Did the forms of participation in community or movement decision-making result in the rethinking and reshaping of the relation between public, communal and private space?
With the demolition of the houses, both decision-making practices and spatial structures drastically changed. But this is only the last step of a long-term transformation of the neighborhood, which I describe as "verticalization." I use this term in two senses: first, to denote the physical restructuring of the environment – the "horizontal city" of the one-story houses was replaced with a vertical estate made of high-rises. Second, to denote a political reorganization of the neighborhood decision-making process: from the old structures of acephalous, informal, though effective, management of the streets, to the centralized form of patronage that the City Council uses to enforce their unilateral decisions over the neighborhood. Space could be modified, privatized, emptied, only after this induced transformation in the process of decision-making is enforced.

Is shared space necessarily communal or are we in need of new terms to describe experiences of collectively shaped and maintained shared space (e.g. common space, liberated space, self-managed space, autonomous space etc.)
Bon Pastor defies typical definitions of common or autonomous space: its residents do not frame their social structures as something that has a political meaning. They just see them as the way things have always been, as something whose disappearance is regretted. But they do see them as a collective endeavor that preserved the unity of the neighborhood from the decadence and conflict that lashed many other parts of the city. So, sometimes it is difficult

to apply typical categories of urban analysis to the neighborhood; I think this is a problem that is linked with the underclass many residents belong to. Most of our concepts emerge from traditions, including Marxism, which always had problems in describing or even accepting the existence of the underclass. I think new words should be invented for these practices: to use words developed in other social sectors can be interpreted as a form of internal colonialism, even if we are talking of the same city.

If "commoning" is a term to describe practices of sharing which directly affect social relations and shape social bonds, do you think that certain aspects of your collective experiences may be described as commoning? What are the most important areas of sharing in a society according to your view?
There isn't a single aspect of life in Bon Pastor that is immune to commoning. If in the 1950s women worked together by bringing their wash-tubs into the streets in front of their houses, just to enjoy time together, today people share their lives in different ways, given the lack and precariousness of jobs, but they are not less dependent on common resources. People rely on neighbors: many have lived very close to each other for decades, and consider themselves "just like families," as they say. They share common memories and practices, ways of behaving, a particular sense of humor, and a general proneness to gossip and share an interest in the lives of their neighbors. This puts local community at the center of people's lives; instead of being an annoying background noise, neighborhood life is an important part of the residents' lives, interests, concerns, and investment of energies. This simple thing makes the whole place very different from the neighborhoods that surround it.

Architecture and alternative urban futures

What was (is) the role of specialists (architects, urban planners, lawyers, economists, public officials etc.) in your community's (or neighborhood's) practices of space-production?
During the struggle against the demolitions, which we had conducted since 2004, we were helped by volunteer architects

and planners, who put their knowledge at the service of our campaign. In 2007 a group of architects from the Technical School of Architecture organized a survey in Bon Pastor to evaluate the status of the houses: they declared that it was possible to refurbish most of them, instead of demolishing them, which the City Council presented as the only solution. Then, from 2010, the project "Repensar Bonpastor" brought hundreds of international experts to Bon Pastor, in order to design alternative solutions for the neighborhood, which didn't involve demolitions and displacements. Most of them were architects or urban planners, and created permanent relations between those residents who were struggling against the demolitions, and the architects who were dissatisfied with the contemporary trend of their discipline, especially concerning urban planning in poor neighborhoods, and the policies of social housing.

Do you see any meaning in the term "emancipating architectures"? Can architecture and urban planning as practices and forms of specialized knowledge assist movement struggles? How? Please refer to examples.
In our case, the presence of architects and urban planners was useful in challenging the official discourse, which described the neighborhood as in a ruinous state, thus justifying the demolitions, and in promoting the idea that other possibilities of intervention exist. They basically expressed in technical language what the residents already knew well: most of them had refurbished their houses for decades, some were masons, and knew the strengths and weaknesses of the construction. Unfortunately, certain insights have to be conveyed in a language that the institutions are able to recognize; here comes the task of technicians and experts. Obviously, in Bon Pastor they made their own observations and studies on the houses, but their position was very close to that of the neighbors.

What is a city for you? How would you define an ideal city? Can there be forms of social organization that will make contemporary metropolises places of sharing and equality? Can such forms give new meaning to everyday habits and everyday problems of survival?

The definition I use to define Bon Pastor is "the horizontal city." It is not the structure of the neighborhood that is horizontal; it is the way local society is conceived, as a network of networks, in which nobody should ever occupy a higher place than another, or pretend to centralize power or control. When everybody lived in the houses, each neighbor had a view over their street and was concerned with what happened outside their house. This individual interest merged with the need of everybody to keep the space under control. But this control could never fall in the hands of a single person or group: information was passed through gossip, from one house to the other, from one street to the other, but nobody occupied a higher place of observation, nobody was really crucial. And when there was a conflict in the street, the whole neighborhood would go out to see what was happening, and eventually to take part in it. There was a collective engagement with local society: something that residents took for granted, when they had it, but when it started to fall they realized that it was something much more precious than the square meters of their new flats, or the solar panels on their new roofs. It was like the "seeds beneath the snow" of traditional anarchist theory: the capacity that normal people have to manage autonomously their space, their lives, their relationships. This is increasingly rare in our cities: the administrations are frightened by places where people are able to self-organize, and strive to take control over them. I think that if residents understood better what they were going to lose with the demolition of the houses, without getting trapped into the allure of "modernity" and into the false dichotomy between "old houses" and "new flats," there might have been a stronger defense of the neighborhood and its features. I hope that this experience, if shared properly, could be useful to other urban communities undergoing the same threat.

What is the role of urban movements in shaping alternative views about city and society?

It depends on what we call urban movements. In Barcelona there have always been strong movements in defense of the right of housing. But often they have difficulties in grasping what happens in the extreme peripheries: most platforms are made of middle-class, idealistic young people, who do a wonderful job in certain neighborhoods, but completely fail to understand the more complex parts of the city. Bon Pastor is hard to comprehend, because people don't speak the language of social movements; they are cynical and ironic, and defy any authority, even the one that activists, unwillingly, sometimes carry in their attitudes. This brought about instances of misunderstanding, which further alienated the neighborhood from the rest of the city. Bon Pastor's residents could never count on external movements to defend their position, except when the group "Repensar Bonpastor" helped them make their story known. Even today, after the great transformation in local politics that resulted in the election of the new mayor of Barcelona, nothing really changed for the neighbor-hood. Surprisingly, the same people who in previous years were the spokespersons of the Socialist Party and of the City Council that promoted the demolition of the neighborhood, now changed their shirts and became the local committee of "Barcelona en Comú"! They support Ada Colau and repeat the slogans of the Indignados, but keep on defending the demolition of the houses, the promotion of mortgages, the construction of new buildings, and the destruction of local culture and ways of life. The problem here, again, is the underclass: no organized movement is brave enough to take a stance in favor of such a diverse, recalcitrant, contradictory population, such as the residents of the extreme peripheries. Maybe, in Barcelona, the last big social movement that had no doubt in defending the most vulnerable sectors of the population was the anarchist workers' union CNT ... but very little is left of that experience.

Can you see in your experiences and struggles elements of a future, more just, society? Do your acts "prefigure," in a way, the future society you long for?
As for seeds beneath the snow, it's only a question of waiting for spring to come; if not this spring, it will be the next one. The story of Bon Pastor will not be forgotten, despite the efforts that the City Council put in it, and will be a source of inspira-

tion for movements of the future. We have to struggle to remove stereotypes and instrumental versions of history, which explain the demolition as if it was done for the sake of the residents, not for the profit of the few. But what was lost in Bon Pastor, this capacity of managing the territory and solving conflicts without referring to external authorities, is something that will surely be recognized as crucial, when we will have to imagine a new city, a new society. We live at a time of quick transformations; more and more people see that a different form of organizing society is needed, different than the one that nation-states had represented until now. By maintaining the memory of what Bon Pastor and these "unruly" parts of the city used to be, where autonomous cultural forms were produced, and by critically relating it to our current situation, we can imagine a "horizontal" city of the future, which can slowly replace the oppressive metropolis we are been pushed to live into.

6

Commoning neighborhoods: the mutual help practices of Brazilian homeless movements

USINA and the *mutirão* tradition

The USINA team from *São Paulo* (Brazil) is a group of architects, planners, economists, and other relevant housing experts that explicitly supports participatory planning and works mainly with homeless movements. One USINA report effectively sums up the logic of this team's interventions: "In the case of urban *mutiroes*, the pedagogical process of social change begins with the people's organization in the struggle for land and access to public funding; it continues with the collective definition of projects and is finally consolidated in stonemasonry" (USINA 2006:17). Homeless workers associations, organized in the context of very active movements struggling for the right to housing, not only participate in the design of their future social housing complexes but are educated by USINA to be able to work in the construction process efficiently and through organized forms of collaboration. These are directly connected to the rich tradition of community cooperation developed in Brazil's rural areas (the *mutirão* tradition) and are considered not only in terms of efficiency but also as instances of building community feeling. Materialization thus acquires an educative role for the members of an emerging community of inhabitants. They are learning as well as discovering how to work and live together, how to create their own common urban environment, and how to support each other.

All this is not outside the realm of architecture as a complex mixture of knowledges, skills, patterns of collaboration between experts, and forms to communication between experts and users. The USINA team proposes a type of building construction based on the prefabrication of the load-bearing structural elements, in order to make it possible for future residents to work as unskilled or low-skilled workers in most of the on-site works. Construction work thus becomes an important part of the participation process. And architecture may indeed contribute to the production of shared common spaces by envisaging construction processes as commoning processes. The resulting common spaces of the USINA projects (among them: common staircases and courtyards open to the dwellers' micro-communities) were not only recognized as such through use but were also symbolically identified with the collectivities of the participating urban commoners.

The history of USINA is directly linked with major changes that took place in Brazilian society during the period of the military regime (1964–1985) and especially after its fall. As Pedro Arantes, one of the current members of USINA, suggests, the rise of social movements in the urban peripheries of São Paulo, and the formation of Partido dos Trabajadores (PT, Workers Party), constitute major politico-social developments in support of the urban and rural poor (Arantes 2013). São Paulo is one of the most divided cities in the world (Caldeira 2000), and the gap between the extra-rich urban elite and the urban population living in the enormous city periphery is unfathomable.

The housing problem is defined as well as encountered in such conditions of social polarization. And it is the homeless and the poorly housed masses that became the most important collective actors in shaping social housing policies in this period. Important social experiments of self-management in the creation of housing areas for these urban populations unfolded mainly due to the pioneer organizational work of urban social movements. As Arantes remarks, "the social struggle of these housing organizations was characterized by the constant shift between confrontation and conciliation, dissension and a desire to integrate" (2013,).

In order to understand the challenges faced by the USINA militant interventions in the housing problem of Brazil some of the defining characteristics of this problem need to be kept in mind, which relate it both to the country's economy and to the socio-cultural divisions that prevail. A country in which the poor are very poor and the rich are very rich, Brazil is also traversed by cultural, religious, and racial discriminations. Capitalist modernization, which advanced at an unprecedented pace mainly after the Second World War, was deeply connected to issues of city management and development as well as to real estate speculation.

An important turning point in the aggressive expansion of this process of modernization was the struggle for a new constitution in 1987. An inclusive social movement called Urban Reform, comprising housing movements, city-rights movements, professional associations, unions, NGOs, Liberation Theology movements, universities and research centers, and groups of progressive mayors was created to promote common demands "including public participation in land use decisions and planning policies" (Maricato 2009: 201). One of Urban Reform's most significant achievements in this struggle was "the inclusion of the social function of property and the social function of the city in the 1988 Brazilian Constitution" (Maricato 2009: 203).

The next turning point was equally decisive in terms of the potentialities it created for the implementation of the right to the city in Brazilian society: The City Statute Federal Law was voted by the National Congress in 2001. This very complex law actually develops the legal tools necessary for the democratization of city governance, the regularization of land ownership (in direct connection to the social function of property established by the 1988 Constitution), the protection of the environment and the development of urban justice policies (Santo Carvalho and Rossbach 2010). In principle the City Statute was opening the road to housing policies in support of those in greater need. However, the legal framework of this law remains today mostly inoperative mainly due to a conservative opposition that expresses the interests of long established socio-economic elites.

As Erminia Maricato, one of the central figures in the Urban Reform struggles and Vice Minister of the newly established Ministry of the Cities (2003–2005) points out in an article written in 2014: "There are two conflicting scenarios at hand: increasing exclusion and social rights, or repeating another chapter of 'conservative modernization.' One of the aspects of this conflicting scenario is the clash between the new legal framework assigning urban rights to everyone, and a reality in which rights are granted only to a few" (Maricato 2016). To this day, the option of conservative modernization seems particularly strong especially in a period in which urban movements are less powerful and the promising administration of PT has proven disappointing for those who hoped for a beyond-neoliberalism future. Nevertheless, policies promoted by progressive PT mayors and supported by struggles for the right to housing have established a tradition that is very much alive in Brazilian cities.

Central to the history of social housing in São Paulo is a term used from 1985 onwards to describe practices of collaboration and self-management connected to housing movements: *mutirão*. "The notion evolved from a term that was used to specify the mutual help amongst farmers during harvest to a broad range of "communal" practices, with collective building as its most remarkable articulation" (Colla et al. 2015: 37). *Mutirão* practices were at the core of the mobilization of urban movements, especially after 1985, becoming both the means to pursue and concretize demands for housing as well as the everyday shared ethics of collective work (during the building construction) and cohabiting.

Mutirão housing projects have acquired different characteristics depending on the changes in housing struggles, the character of the housing movements involved and the political history of Brazil. A crucial turning point in the history is the rise of PT to power in the São Paulo municipality (1989). The new administration of Luiz Erundina and the new head of the Housing and Urban Development Department, Professor Erminia Maricato, actually established a housing program based on self-managed cooperative production (Arantes 2004: 194), a local state-supported *mutirão* program, one might say. Different forms and levels of negotiation of housing movements with the new administration resulted in a whole range of publicly funded social housing projects.

The pioneer Uruguayan model of housing cooperatives

Of crucial importance for the tradition of self-managed housing in Latin America is the pioneer work of FUCVAM (*Federacion Uruguaya de Cooperativas de Vivienda por Ayuda Mutua* – Uruguayan Federation of Housing Cooperatives through Mutual Help). As engineer Benjamin Nahoum, one of the Federation's central figures, explains, the establishment of the Uruguayan models begins with the National Housing Law voted upon in 1968 (*Ley* 13.728). According to Nahoum, the power and innovative character of this model stem from an original combination of elements which predated the law but were mutually strengthened by becoming linked in this institutional frame (Nahoum 2015: 38). Those elements were: the tradition of self-management (*autogestion*) very much present in many forms of everyday collaboration and closely linked to the cooperativist tradition (both in Uruguay and all over the world); the customary forms of personal contribution (*aporte propio*), and mutual help (*ayuda mutua*) connected to practices of cooperation in both rural and urban contexts (in the tradition of auto-construction widely developed in Latin American cities especially by the urban poor); and the form of collective ownership, which although legally non-existent in Uruguay until 1968, "is one to the oldest American traditions" (Nahoum 2015: 38).

Although this law explicitly addressed the problem of housing production as an urgent social need, its implications were even more important in establishing organized communities of urban commoners. The power of those communities and the influence of mutual help ethos were directly demonstrated in 1984 when the Uruguayan dictatorship tried to strike at the heart of the cooperative movement by abolishing collective ownership (Castro et al. 2012); 330,000 signatures were collected in just one day explicitly denouncing the change of the law (Machado 2016). Due to this mobilization the dictatorship abandoned its plans (Machado 2016: 35). "In that day FUCVAM, that was leading the struggle, became the symbol of the resistance against the dictatorship" (Nahoum 2015: 40). Cooperative assemblies, thus, remained nuclei of collective deliberation in a period in which public gatherings were prohibited and activists were chased by the junta.

Uruguayan cooperatives, and especially those based on mutual help (which form FUCVAM), are based on practices of commoning that acquire emancipatory characteristics. These characteristics develop unevenly depending on the differences in the socio-historical context of each specific project but it seems that all of them combine *productive efficiency* with *pedagogic motivation* and *prefigurative opportunities.*

Productive efficiency has to do with organizational choices. Combining forces and using each and everyone's skills and abilities (either already advanced or developing ones) is what makes collective work efficient. In the many cases in which a specific union of workers took the initiative of forming a housing cooperative (Nahoum 2015: 43), the union's organizational experience played an important role. Collective action and knowledge that were developed through struggle made people aware of the problems connected to the distribution of tasks within a group characterized by its adherence to a specific scope.

In all of its modalities related to different contexts, the problem of organization of a cooperative's production process is closely connected to the problem of power distribution. And power structures develop or are challenged on every level of this process: at the level of decision-making; at the level of negotiations with state and funding institutions; at the level of relations with the Technical Assistance Institutes (*Institutos de Asistencia Tecnica*); at the level of coordination between cooperative members who take part in mutual help labor; and at the level of management of the construction site as well as the housing complex after it is completed. As suggested throughout this book, the organizing of commoning directly reflects relations of power. A potentially emancipating commoning process needs to be based on relations of horizontality and power sharing.

Uruguayan housing cooperatives, according to the *Ley de Vivienda*, have as the supreme organ of decision-making the general assembly. It is this assembly that elects the Directory Committee which is bound to the assembly's decisions and directives (Decree 633/69). Of course, institutional obligations may

create opportunities of democracy but only the engaged participation of people along with an ethos of solidarity and equality can
perform democracy as praxis.

The difficult problem is how to connect efficiency with democratic deliberation. Key to the innovative contribution of the
Uruguayan cooperative experiences to this problem's solution
is the combination of participation in decision-making with
the organized participation in the construction works. Different
models seem to have been developed in Uruguay and Brazil for
connecting rights and obligations in such a process. Generally
speaking, mutual help cooperatives require their members to
contribute to the construction on an equal basis as workers.
Because most of them work, the contribution of men develops
especially during the afternoon hours (after work) or during the
weekends. Women who do not work outside their house may also
contribute during weekdays.

Interestingly, *ayuda mutua* projects give future inhabitants the
opportunity to collaborate with construction workers of different
specialties who are employed by the cooperative. The fact that
the housing construction is not simply contracted to an enterprise makes the construction site an experiment of collectively
self-managed work. Thus, relations stemming from division of
labor are not taken for granted but become the focus of debate
and organizational decisions with impacts on the structure of the
cooperative.

The aforementioned law explicitly establishes the role of the
so-called *Institutos de Asistencia Tecnica* (IAT). These include
architects, economists, social scientists, planners, and other professionals who can be of help in the different tasks of the cooperative, including the design and production of houses (Nahoum
2013: 49–53). In the case of USINA, technical assistance is not
only a technical problem. The way it is provided, the way it
empowers (or disempowers) people in their role as the ultimate
decision-makers, and the way it actually helps people to learn
how to organize mutual help directly affects the distribution of
power within the commoning process. No matter how explicitly
the law and the decrees that followed describe the roles and obligations of various cooperative organs and IAT, the actual process

depends on the political awareness of all those involved. That is why USINA's pioneer work is both architecturally and politically important, and that is why in Brazil the emancipating potentialities of housing cooperativism are closely depended upon the movement that has developed the corresponding association.

Concerning the educative aspect of the Uruguayan cooperative practices *ayuda mutua* participants actually learn how to perform specific tasks in the context of an organized production site. What is more, however, they learn how to work together and how to cooperate in solidarity. It makes a big difference to work with people that are your future neighbors. Empowerment seems to go hand in hand with politicization in Uruguayan cooperatives. Learning their rights and developing their demands for decent living in an inclusive city goes hand in hand with experiencing the power of solidarity and collective struggle.

From the first days of its establishment, FUCVAM was part of the movement. Not only has it resisted the anti-popular plans of the dictatorship but has also strengthened the mutual support networks developed through cooperative action. Actually, in Uruguay *cooperativismo* became a strong movement that educated people in the values of self-management and sharing. "Because, as goes the song written by Ruben Olivera for the cooperatives that was transformed to a hymn, 'houses are the beginning, not the end'" (Nahoum 2015: 42).

Starting from this last emblematic verse, one can explore the prefigurative elements of Uruguayan *cooperativismo*. Surely these have to do with the inspiring effect of the cooperative values: cooperation, mutual support, participation in democratic decision-making practices. But what makes the FUCVAM model a potential challenge to established social relations (including economic ones) is the status of collective property. As explicitly defined by the 1968 law, the members of the cooperative are collectively (and not individually) responsible for the payment of the loan obtained for the construction of the housing project, as well as for the maintenance of the houses. Each member family signs an agreement with the cooperative that gives it the right of "use and enjoyment" (*"uso y goce"*) for a specific apartment (Nahoum 2015: 46).

Members belong to a community which shares rights and obligations. If a family cannot afford to pay its share of the loan for a certain period, the cooperative may cover the debt. And if members decide to leave, they can only receive back in money the value invested in the project by their work and loan share payments. This makes it possible to protect the housing complex from speculation pressures.

Obviously common property is a huge prefigurative accomplishment of the Uruguayan cooperatives and especially of FUCVAM. A document published by the National Direction of FUCVAM in 2011 states: "The cooperatives following the FUCVAM model are a problem for the system (capitalism) and today, given that yesterday's opposition is now in government, we are a problem for those who previously supported us. Nothing has changed in our plans, only the scenery has changed" (Castro et al. 2012: 45).This document actually refers to the disillusionment of the cooperative movement caused by the gradual adaptation by the progressive *Frente Amplio* government (in power from 2005) of market oriented housing policies.

Collective property gives new meaning to the housing complex's spaces. These spaces become "a true extension of the houses, which not only augments the spaces of private use, thus producing better life quality, but also transforms them to a true center of the neighborhood's social life" (Nahoum 2015: 47).

Collective property produces a context of social relations within the cooperative that favors collective appropriation of shared resources (including the neighborhood's facilities) and an ethos of commoning. Realizing that what they can share and develop is based on use value and not on exchange value gives cooperative members an important opportunity to transcend dominant ideologies based on individual profit alone. Of course, the property status of the houses does not simply convert the cooperative neighborhoods to emancipated equalitarian communities. Lots of different relations based on established and perpetuated asymmetries (including political affiliation and union leadership modes) interfere in the geometries of power within the cooperative. However, if commoning needs to be based on mechanisms of power sharing, if it is to gesture towards an emancipated society, then the status of collective property is a powerful mechanism of such kind. What in many Latin American countries is called "social production of housing" acquires in Uruguay a remarkably distinctive characteristic: the guaranteed social *use* and social *management* of housing is based on the social value (as distinct from market value) of property. Comparably (albeit in a way that is very limited in its challenge to prevailing approaches to individual property), the Brazilian Constitution of 1988 states that "property shall observe its social function" (art. 5(XXIII)). This article was especially used by homeless and landless movements to defend their occupations in courts by insisting that they use abandoned properties with no social function.

It is important to know that collective property status in Uruguayan housing cooperatives can change according to decisions taken by the cooperative's general assembly. As the law and relevant decrees state, after the complete payment of the loan (which, let us remember, is a collective responsibility) the cooperative may decide either to keep the status of collective property and assign to each family rights of use, or attribute individual property rights to each cooperative member-inhabitant (Castro et al. 2012: 35). The dynamics of emancipatory commoning (including the dynamics contained in the collective property status) depend on the level of politicized engagement of the cooperative members as well as on the socio-historical context of the cooperative's actions.

The Uruguayan housing cooperatives model exerts a long-lasting influence in Latin American countries (Olsson 2011, Nahoum 2015). Especially in Brazil this influence can be traced back to the first *mutirão* projects of the early 1980s in the state of São Paulo (e.g. the Vila Comunitaria), as one of the involved pioneer architects remembers – Leonardo Pessina, a Uruguayan émigré, self-exiled in Amsterdam, who came to Brazil in 1982 (Pessina 2016: 18–19).

Compared to the Uruguayan relevant experience of self-managed housing production (which for some was the initial inspiring origin of Brazilian housing *mutirão*, see Arantes 2004: 192), the Brazilian projects have an important difference.

In the Uruguayan case, the buildings are owned by the dwelling cooperative, generally related to syndicates and social movements. They receive funding from the state and pay it back collectively to the state. This results in a collective property in which the inhabitants pay a monthly rent. In the Brazilian case the movement creates a community association to build a housing project. Works are done with public funds and the houses become property of the inhabitants, who must pay the funding back to the government. (Colla et al. 2015: 83)

Due to this fundamental difference with the Uruguayan institutional context, relations with local and central state develop unevenly. The "constant shift between confrontation and conciliation" to which Arantes refers should be understood as the necessary result of such power relations. *Mutirão* projects had, at times of great mobilization, become emblematic of struggles for social emancipation, whereas in other cases they have been assimilated to state "welfare" policies without challenging their limitations.

In this complicated history, the role played by multidisciplinary working groups like USINA is important. Recognized by the state as *assesorias tecnicas*, they offered "architectural and technical support for the design and construction of cooperative popular building projects" (Colla et al. 2015: 54). Founded in 1990, USINA remains faithful to the initial, socially engaged scopes of militant technical advisory offices, whereas other similar groups evolved into private architectural firms.

Challenging the established role of design

In order to understand the contribution of USINA's wok to the rethinking of housing design and production considered as a commoning process we need to connect it to an important discussion about the role of design that is been going on in Brazil since the 1970s. As part of a self-reflexive and socially engaged architectural modernism, this discussion has been crucially influenced by the contributions of Sergio Ferro. An important architect, academic, artist, and activist, Ferro has essentially focused his criticism of architectural practice, or the "architectural mode of production," as he prefers to call it, on the relation of design to the construction site. Starting from a Marxist analysis of the construction site as a production area, Ferro focuses especially on the conditions of labor: being different both from handicraft production relations as well as from the industrial ones, the building site "is fundamentally characterized by the essential operational role of the labour power" (2016: 95). Ferro suggests that construction remains relatively less industrialized and less technologically advanced than other sectors of production because it relies essentially on the extraction of surplus value directly from labor: it is not by chance that today (almost 50 years after Ferro introduced these thoughts) construction is still a locomotive-type sector of economy in developing capitalist countries, especially in Asia and Latin America, which is based on the grave exploitation of millions of workers. It is a process which, among other means and policy decisions, "is used by capital to fight against its worst nightmare: the inevitable tendency of the rate of profit to fall with the constant advance of the productive forces" (Ferro 2016: 95–96).

Labor power, trapped in the construction site by the capitalist command, cannot organize itself as the true producer of the building, for which it employs skills acquired through practice and knowledges not transferred to machines and automated systems (as happens in more advanced sectors of production). "Totalisation, that is, [the] integration [of specialized teams of laborers] as elements in forming the common product (i.e. the building or the bridge), is the exclusive function of the capital that acquired the diverse labor powers allotted to the teams" (Ferro 2016: 96). Totalization, thus, remains external to labor. It is the "worker's cooperatives," the "collective worker, the productive body" (Ferro 2016: 97) organized as a force which reclaims the production and its product, that shows the way towards a "totalising" process of labor's "self-determination" (Ferro 2016: 97).

Ferro's most controversial suggestion is that design actually assumes the role of corroborating capital's command in construction production by being completely disengaged both from the building site and the laborer's shared knowledges and skills. That is why essentially "Design ... proceeds to seek in itself or in its history, forms that were external to the laborer's range of forms" (Ferro 2016: 100). "But the separation between design and building site impedes any confrontation in a mutual, autonomous training process, in which design and building site might be able to dialogue, and so correct the proclivity of autism in separated design" (Ferro 2016: 101). Clearly this is a radical criticism of architectural practice and its social role. As the architectural critic and historian Hugo Segawa describes it:

> One cannot dissociate the set of statements by Sergio Ferro from the intellectual context of the 1968 events ... His observations are related to the analyses that French philosophers, including Michel Foucault (1926–1984), developed in order to criticize the deformations of modernity, the repressive rationalism, and the positivistic teleology of modernism. However, in Brazil, his ideas were deemed the word of order against the project, namely, the defense of the 'non-project.' Making the architecture project meant endorsing the system, corroborating the dictatorship; rejecting the project meant boycotting the current 'mode of architectural production,' which should be replaced." (Segawa 2013: 184)

Ferro's approach is a radical rethinking of design as a practice related to the conditions of space production as well as to the conditions of work in construction sites. From this approach a rethinking of the problem of collective housing has emerged in which the reclaiming of the product by the potential users (inhabitants) was strongly connected to a reclaiming of the production process (construction). In what came to be known as *mutirão* housing, people organized in relevant movements were simultaneously involved in the design process, as workers in construction, as members of assemblies which organized work and scopes related to the final product, and as future inhabitants with rights and aspirations.

It is through Ferro's work that we can understand why it was so important for USINA to develop its contribution to the *mutirão* housing projects in three distinct complementary directions.

1. In devising tools that would enable participants to form and express opinions about future private and shared spaces (a process explicitly connected to pedagogic scopes as discussed below)

2. In introducing construction methods and materials that would enable *mutirantes* to participate in the construction process, to understand and manage it, and thus resume control over the "totality" of the product, becoming a re-united "productive body" (to use Ferro's terms).
3. In supporting potentialities for new social relations and new forms of organized cohabitation that are meant to be explored through collective experiences developed throughout the entire process of *mutirão*.

All three directions lead to a redefinition of housing through commoning and as commoning.

Commoning the plans

As Pedro Arantes explains in his interview included in this chapter, urban movements need to be "urban experimenters" and "urban dreamers." This means that they need to be offered the means and opportunities to dream of different possible spaces and to experiment with different spatialities and human relations. One needs to be educated, to be able to develop these capacities, to creatively think about and experience space. But this kind of education is not like the authoritarian education which perpetuates the division between manual and intellectual labor and hierarchies connected to knowledge and social position. It is an educating process based explicitly on Freire's *Pedagogy of the Oppressed* (2005): "We defend self-management in the production of inhabited environment as a process of popular education" (USINA 2015: 167)

Part of this process is focused on rethinking the limits and redefining the characteristics of the so-called "private" and "public" realm. One way of doing this is by collectively reflecting on shared experiences of inhabiting. On the level of the shared family realm, a realm of shared privacy to be clearly demarcated from an "outside," interesting new proposals emerged due especially to the contribution of women. Empowered through the participatory process women ask for a different distribution and hierarchy of the house spaces: larger and centrally placed kitchen-and-eating areas (Arantes 2013: 11) corroborate the family's togetherness under the recognized central role of women. Furthermore, everyday common use spaces (such as staircases and entrances) are demanded to be not simply transitory spaces in a circulation system but real meeting places of cohabitants.

In the case of the COPROMO housing complex (Osasco in São Paulo), the staircase was designed as an ample outdoor vertical circulation core directly leading to family apartment balconies on both sides. The resulting spaces are both private and open to occasional public encounters, as balcony users become part of the everyday choreographies of the stairs. A kind of common space is performed thus with the explicit aid of design. And gradual transitions to more private areas (including the part of the apartment meant for the family's social life) unfold in a delicate and nuanced network of threshold spaces (Germano Wagner, USINA architect, interviewed by the author).

Collectively organized participation seems to have challenged a tradition deeply rooted in the cultures of the urban poor. What James Holston describes as the "aesthetics of autoconstruction" (1991: 456) is actually a way of treating the house that people usually build themselves at the city's peripheries as an expression of their distinct family identity. This expressive declaration,

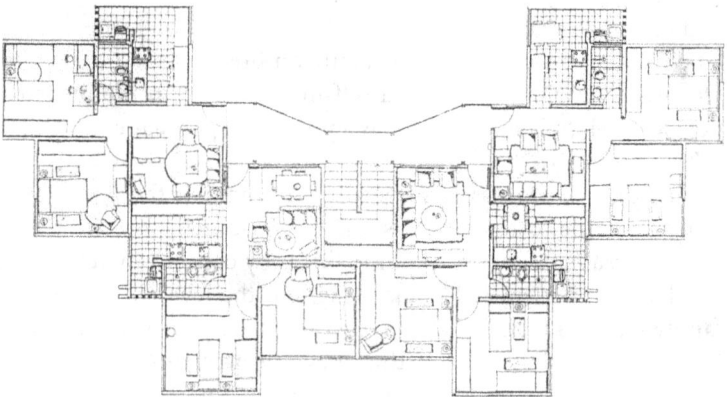

6.1 Plan of a characteristic floor in Osasco complex, São Paulo: balconies as shared spaces

6.2 A network of common spaces connected by the open air shared staircase

mainly transmitted through the house façade, is an act of "aesthetic discrimination" (Holston 1991: 458) that may be considered to promote an individualistic ethos as opposed to a shared community culture that is predominant among the poor in rural areas. It is as if the urban poor are trapped in the hegemonic culture of distinction which asks people to be ostentatiously different from their neighbors. The *mutirão* design process does not aim to eliminate differences or particularities, rather, through collective deliberation in long meetings in which plans are discussed and developed with the help of the USINA architects, flexible space typologies are being invented. So differentiation and individuation develop along the paths of collaboration and sharing. As already seen in the history of the Bon Pastor social housing, collective inventiveness produces and supports differences within the collectively fabricated world of everyday urban commoning.

The means employed to assist people in developing proposals for their family apartments and relevant typologies for the housing buildings were also experience based. In certain cases

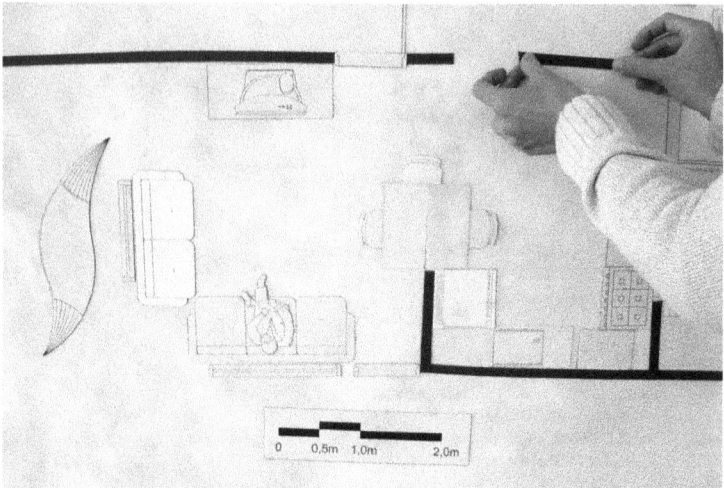

6.3 Practicing participatory design in Tânia Maria and Cinco de Dezembro Complex, Suzano, State of São Paulo

flexible models which could be assembled in different combinations were used (as, for example, in the case of the participatory design of Comuna D. Hélder Câmara in the state of São Paulo).

In the case of the Suzano complex including Mutirões Tânia Maria and Cinco de Dezembro (Suzano is a municipality included in the metropolitan region of São Paulo), the USINA team decided to use actual images of furniture pieces at 1:10 scale (attached to magnets), through which groups of families could explore possible arrangements of their apartments: instead of starting with minimum abstract dimensions, types of apartments were developed out of images of possible spaces, which people could easily apprehend and inventively use (Higuchi et al. 2015). "It is through furniture that the abstract space takes on concrete, lived meaning" (Arantes 2013: 10).

Concerning spaces of public use, a rich process of discussions and assembly decisions gives future inhabitants the opportunity to think differently about the realm of the common. In São Paulo, it is quite common to see gated housing areas not only for the most affluent but also in low-income suburbs or social housing complexes. In some cases USINA proposals were to succumb to the growing demand for securitized housing environment (for example in *Mutirão* União da Juta). However, in direct support of people's aspirations for a more open relation to the surrounding neighborhood, in the Suzano complex, some really innovative proposals for shared spaces came up. Instead of designing an inner courtyard to be used only by the residents of the complex, a choice was made to connect it to the surrounding sidewalk, "forming a public square that the whole neighborhood can use" (Arantes 2013: 12). Common space in this case, has become an area of exchanges with the surrounding urban tissue, instead of being equated with a self-enclosed communal space clearly distinguished from urban public spaces.

Commoning in the construction site

The USINA team understands the construction process not simply as a matter of technology and management, but, essentially following Ferro's critical legacy, as a production process based on laborers' exploitation and alienation that needs to be contested. The participation of future inhabitants as workers in the construction works of their housing complex is the most important step in an effort to create different conditions of labor. The alienation of construction workers from the product of their work is challenged by the direct appropriation of this product by themselves as inhabitants. Also, becoming aware of the difficulties and interdependencies of different tasks, learning how to participate in them and, in certain cases, a rotation in duties, gives to *mutirantes* the real power to collectively control the process (in place of capital's control in usual social housing construction sites). During the construction work, thus, future inhabitants are not only employed as workers (salaries and additional volunteer work depend on the particularities of the project) but also acquire skills they can use in future work. What, however, is more important is that through collective work management they learn that knowledge, skills, organizational methods, and technologies are not independent of value choices: through collaboration, through commoning work (and by working according to commoning values), people learn how to shape and check common tasks and how to develop sharing relations.

The mutual help construction site becomes the most concrete illustration of the threshold character of potentially emancipatory commoning practices: an area of negotiations is being shaped by rules devised through assembly participation, and directly tested in action (threshold rules that are open to deliberation and not imposed by external authorities); subjects of action actually transform themselves through their participation in collaborative work (threshold subjects experiencing transitions in everyday roles); knowledge sharing develops in and through collaboration (through the crossing of thresholds between abstract knowledge and applied skills); ritualized actions of empowerment for *mutirantes*, including feasts, make the construction site a place where new social relations are being performed (thresholds separate but at the same time connect work and leisure, discipline and play, house building and community building).

Technology itself and construction methods need also to be problematized according to this critical approach. What kind of technology would really give *mutirantes* the means to control the construction and labor activities? The construction system proposed by USINA since their first projects in 1990 has proven to be an ingenious solution to complicated construction problems. This system is based on the construction, at the beginning of the building complex's production, of metal stair towers which will be the corresponding vertical circulation cores for the housing buildings. Those metal towers are made of pre-fabricated elements which are assembled in situ. The advantage of this choice

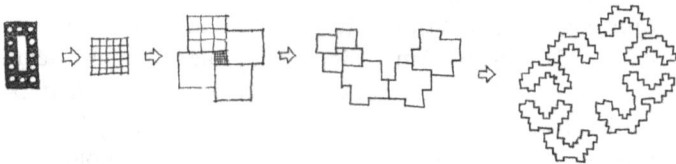

6.4 A design and construction logic based on the idea that unskilled *mutirantes* play a crucial role

6.5 Construction site of building complex in Osasco, São Paulo: prefabricated elements mounted on site to create the stairwell which then becomes a scaffold for the construction of building walls

6.6 Outdoor common space in Osasco complex

is that from the beginning of the works a scaffold is there to assist the erection of the brick loadbearing walls produced out of ceramic structural blocks. Thus, low-skilled workers can work on the building of the walls more easily, while the technologically demanding parts of the construction (including staircases) are already in place. This construction system in a way empowers low-skilled workers, giving them the opportunity to have a total view of the process without losing the opportunity to profit from advances in construction technology. As Arantes states: "Our goal is to find coherence and correspondence between the product and the process of producing it, so that one reinforces the other, rather than deny it" (Arantes 2013: 14).

Commoning as a force of social experimentation

Potentialities for reformed social relations come to the fore during the entire *mutirão* process. Collaboration combined with collective self-management explicitly challenges both the capital command in the construction site and the dominant models of social housing conditions. By being encouraged as well as supported in their efforts to think about the spaces they need while becoming an organized collectivity, participants explicitly or implicitly tackle the major problems of social organization. As seen, USINA's contribution to this process is multileveled. It is central to USINA's political orientation to approach the projects as both a concrete response to today's pressing exigencies (the need for housing) and as an experimental practice of developing alternative models of living and working together. Thus, "The mutirões are embryos of a kind of counter-space, in the words of French philosopher Henri Lefebvre. They exist as the residual virtualities within the planned and programmed order" (Arantes 2013: 6. Compare with Lefebvre's approach to urban virtualities discussed in chapter 1).

If spatial potentialities support creative explorations of possible human relations, as has been already suggested in this book, then USINA's participatory projects can be interpreted as contributions to the potentialization of social housing space through *mutirão*. If at the center of the *mutirão* tradition is the idea of mutual help as an effective and realistic process of accomplishing tasks that would be otherwise impossible for the urban and rural poor, then the transplanting of the relevant ethos to the USINA-assisted laboratories of social emancipation converts it to a potentializing factor both of space and of society. *Mutirão*, in this context, becomes part of commoning practices. Mutual help becomes the propelling force of organized collaboration as well as of organized coexistence. True, lots of obstacles need to be confronted in those social housing commoning projects, prevailing capitalist relations being the strongest generators of them. Dealing with knowledge deficit or with the denigration of popular knowledges and skills is obviously one of them. Faith in the power of architectural design to transform social relations has in Brazil, as in many countries, misguided modernist architects. As one of them boldly stated back in the 1970s in Brazil: "we are able to identify the social project through the design [*desenho*]. And with it we will find the right language in order to conduct human emancipation" (Motta 1975: 29 as cited in Segawa 2013: 174).

This approach directly emphasizes the role of the architect, who "knows" and has the appropriate education, as the central strategist of social change. And of course this approach reproduces the disempowerment of the people as well as their skepticism (if not outward hostility) towards "enlightened" intellectuals.

USINA, by basing themselves on the critical tradition of Sergio Ferro among others, refused to assume this role. Instead they chose to become catalysts in practices of collaboration which involved exchanges of knowledge(s) as well as experiences and aspirations. Trusting the power of commoning as a potentially liberating process that challenges established classifications of duties and competencies is at the center of USINA's ethics and concrete proposals. And, as Ferro himself confesses in his introduction to a book commemorating USINA's 25 years of work: "my sympathies with the anarchist tactics of direct action in the production sites too incline me to admire [USINA] with great humility, for my own activity has never reached the happy symbiosis between the admirable daring and competence of USINA and the tenacious courage of the dispossessed and their organizations with which they share revolutionary hope" (Ferro 2015: 29–30). Thus,

"The experience of USINA clearly demonstrates that, despite the uninterrupted adversity it encounters, another exercise of architecture is possible today and here. And it makes us hope that … it is possible to accelerate the always delayed arrival of tomorrows that sing – before we become deaf" (Ferro 2015: 30).

Interview with Pedro Arantes, architect, urbanist, member of USINA collective and professor at the Universidade Federal de São Paulo, 27 July 2016 (author's translation)

Public space, common space

How is public space produced in the settlement you have designed?
Who decides – what are the practices of such space production?
When we design housing complexes together with the future inhabitants all issues are discussed in the project assemblies. Matters concerning the house interiors, the semi-private areas, the common spaces, and the public spaces. Public space matters are also discussed with the region's secretaries if the provision of public services is involved. Unfortunately such collaborative meetings don't always take place so we predominantly design the communal spaces that are created by the inhabitants and their associations.

Please refer to some crucial events that shaped your views and proposals about public and private space in housing areas.
International experiences that constitute reference points for us are: Viennese courtyard housing (Hof), some of the new German Siedlungen of the Weimar period, participatory design housing projects of the 1960s and 1970s (Giancarlo di Carlo, Van Eyck, Herman Hertzenberger, Ralph Erskine, Lucien Kroll), SAAL projects in Portugal (Siza, Portas etc), critical regionalism in Spain and Italy, the work of John Turner and the mutual help project, Hasan Fathy's work in Egypt, FUCVAM in Uruguay, community architects, and Cuban Brigadas. Brazilian experiences: Cajueiro Seco (in Recife during the 1960s – Acácio Gil Borsói), Bras de

Pina (Carlos Nelson dos Santos), Pedregulho (Reidy e Carmem Portinho), projects developed during the re-democratization period (during the 1980s: Vila Nova Cachoerinha, Vila Comunitária de São Bernardo, Recanto da Alegria), student housing in Unicamp (Nudecri), *mutirão* projects in São Paulo (especially during the period of the Erudina – PT administration from 1989 to 1992).

Please describe the ways of decision-making in terms of the settlement's layout, the rules of building and the regulations of the settlement's maintenance (in one or two cases of your projects).
It depends on the specific case. In USINA we have produced all kinds of projects in differing contexts.

What does it mean for you to share space? What is the meaning of private space for you?
Shared space is divided between many families. Private space is space for a single family.

How do the communities you work with organize themselves? Are we talking about a stable community, an expanding community?
In Brazil communities are never stable. Families become larger, work mobility creates changes, so does social mobility (ascending or descending), and the abandoning of the family house for various reasons (illness, intra-family violence, drug dealing violence etc.).

Please describe the ways you have approached the problem of social inequality. Do you think that inequality is being shaped differently in cities than in rural areas? Is there any meaning for you in the term "spatial justice"?
Yes, the term spatial justice is classic in reference to struggles for the right to the city. In Brazil, successes were greater in rural areas, with a partial agrarian reform and a powerful and well organized social movement, the MST (Movimento dos Trabalhadores Rurais Sem Terra, Landless Rural Workers Movement). In cities inequalities are larger, confrontations more prominent and social movements more fragmented. It is more difficult to reverse social

inequalities because they are multileveled and many of the relevant factors are beyond the reach of popular movements. In rural areas, in the settlements of agrarian reform, movements have greater capacity to change conditions concerning living, work, education, relations with nature etc.

Did you collectively draw examples for self-management from shared traditions? Is collective memory a source for social experiments of collaboration? In what way?
This is more usual in projects we realize in rural areas, in which a stronger memory concerning past forms of living and production persists, a memory of popular knowledge connected to agriculture and construction skills as well as memories concerning the originary people [populações originárias] (natives). In urban areas all this is lost.

Sharing and commoning

Do you think it is important to develop practices of sharing in and through space? How?
Yes it is crucial. Examples include communal gardens, urban agriculture, children and youth spaces, small cultural and sports centers, shared-use vehicles. In one of our housing projects, the *mutirão* Paulo Freire, we even managed to create a community bank with social currency (*Moeda Social*).

Did the forms of participation in community or movement decision-making result in the rethinking and reshaping of the relation between public, communal, and private space?
Yes, the more organized a community is in taking shared decisions (knowing how to organize its actions in a collective way, based on horizontality and democracy), the more this community will be prepared to develop communication experiences and public ones. In less organized communities there is a tendency for each one to close oneself in one's private spaces and not to construct common spaces and solidarity bonds.

Is shared space necessarily communal or are we in need of new terms to describe experiences of collectively shaped and maintained shared space (e.g. common space, liberated space, self-managed space, autonomous space etc.)

In Brazil we use all of these terms depending on the context and the group we work with. With urban movements we more often talk about self-managed spaces. With rural movements we usually refer to autonomous or liberated spaces. The meaning, however, is more or less the same.

If "commoning" is a term to describe practices of sharing which directly affect social relations and shape social bonds, do you think that certain aspects of your collective experiences may be described as commoning? What are the most important areas of sharing in a society according to your view?

Yes, almost all of the work of USINA takes place at the area of the common, both at the interface of communities and inside them. As I have already said, in our projects movements construct not only houses: schools and nursery stations, community centers, community bakeries, cultural centers, squares, sports areas, gardens, urban agricultural areas, etc ... In the agrarian reform settlements they also construct space of production: silos, storehouses, agricultural industry installations etc.

Architecture and alternative urban futures

What was (is) the role of specialists (architects, urban planners, lawyers, economists, public officials etc.) in practices of space-production?

Depending on the context we either have conflicts or collaboration between the movements and the communities on one side and the experts on the other. The so-called technical advisors [*asesorias tecnicas*] (USINA and other groups such as Peabiru, Instituto Polis, Centro Gaspar Garcia, Ambiente, to mention a few from São Paolo) are formed by specialists who are partners with social movements. Concerning relations with local governments, in depends largely on the party that is in power at the time as well as on its corresponding politicians for the specialists to be able or not to empower self-management and communitarian practices.

Do you see any meaning in the term "emancipating architectures"? Can architecture and urban planning as practices and forms of specialized knowledge assist movement struggles? How? Please refer to examples.
Emancipation – social and individual – is a multidimensional and complicated process. Architecture and urban design play a role in emancipatory processes, albeit not a protagonist one.

Modern architects always had the illusion that new spaces construct new relations; however, it is from new relations that new spaces are being induced. Emancipating relations are shaped by the ways communities are empowered in order to decide how to live, by their forms of governing, by democracy, by cultural production etc. The best and most radical projects which USINA has realized were not the result of its architects' abilities but of the corresponding community's knowledge and determination to produce its spaces with imagination, dignity, and justice.

What is a city for you? How would you define an ideal city? Can there be forms of social organization that will make contemporary metropolises places of sharing and equality? Can such forms give new meaning to everyday habits and everyday problems of survival?
This question would deserve a course or a book to be answered. Possible definitions are many and they depend on the contingencies and historical conjectures, as well as on the condition of class and power relations which support it. Since the 1960s, critical thinking has progressed a lot in defining the urban and its contradictions. But, in order not to evade the question: for me the city is at the same time the process and the product of social, cultural, and economic relations of societies in determined territories. It is for this reason that the city is the materialization in buildings, infrastructures, and environmental dimensions of the social and production relations themselves. This is why the analysis of the city history and of the urban landscape is so rich and instigating; it permits, starting from the built environment, a reading of

relations which would otherwise be invisible. The city provides history with materiality because historical layers that are usually ignored become visible and so do equalities and inequalities.

It is obvious that an ideal city would be the reflection of an ideal society. Many great utopias had an urban form: Thomas More's *Utopia*, Sir Francis Bacon's *New Atlantis*, William Morris's ideal city described in his work *News from Nowhere*, Le Corbusier's ideal modern cities, Constant's *New Babylon* to mention a few. However, when [utopias] were actually built, as in the case of Chandigarh or Brasilia, they became their opposite: they were realized in conditions of degrading manual labor, social exclusion, violence, and segregation. Urban utopias can easily turn to heterotopias or dystopias. Or can even become "evil paradises," as Mike Davis has named the cities that contemporary neoliberal capitalism is dreaming of, the most prominent examples being those constructed in the Arabian Emirates.

What is the role of urban movements in shaping alternative views about city and society?
Urban movements no doubt play an important role as urban experimenters and as urban dreamers (imagineers, *imaginadores urbanos*), to use David Harvey's term. The radical critique of the city of capital must be accompanied by spaces of hope, spaces where new social relations are constructed that imply new urban forms and the process that produces them. New visions of society will be shaped only by testing alternatives and not by simply waiting for a revolutionary liberating process to come.

Can you see in your experiences and struggles elements of a future, more just, society? Do your acts "prefigure," in a way, the future society you long for?
Together with the communities and the movements with which the USINA collective has worked and still works, we always try to realize in every project, in every work, a prefiguration of another city, more just, more solidarity-based, more beautiful. Prefiguration is especially focused on the empowerment of subjects, considered as producer-thinkers of cities, capable of imagining different futures. One of the disasters that capitalism and

consumer society has inflicted upon us is the sterilization of the capacity to imagine alternatives. Populations become hostages to the utopias of capital, they are trapped by fancy advertisements and lose the capacity to glimpse at other possible worlds, to imagine more just societies, while considering the rules of the game that capital imposes as natural. It is fundamental to reclaim urban imagination, through those prefigurations, no matter how partial they may be.

7

Commoning neighborhoods: building autonomy in Mexico City

Self-managed housing and emancipating inventiveness

The housing question in Mexico (and probably in most Latin American metropolises) is directly connected to major challenges to the dominant urban order. Socially marginalized or excluded populations face not only chronic joblessness but also extremely precarious housing conditions. Usually forced to the peripheries of megacities, such populations are either dependent upon ruthless landlords, who charge extreme rents for miserable apartments, or have to improvise in building a shelter in illegal or semi-illegal settlements (*favelas*, *villas miserias*, etc.)

In such a context, practices of cooperation and collective work are very important for the urban poor. As Esteva remarks, the poor can only survive if they combine their efforts, if they devise ways to share scarce resources and even scarcer means to use those resources, whereas the middle classes or the rich can still reproduce themselves by obstinately clinging to individualism (Esteva 2015).

Sharing and urban commoning, thus, are not practices chosen out of ideological preferences but, rather, essential ways to ensure a somewhat bearable life for those people. However, through those practices, and by evaluating the experiences linked to them, the urban poor learn how to take their lives in their hands, how to organize their communities as shared worlds. Commoning implicitly or explicitly politicizes the excluded populations: it shows them ways to different social relations, ways to different economic relations, and ways to different forms of common life that depart from dominant individualist principles.

Important experiments of urban commoning and collective self-management have unfolded in the peripheries of one of the largest cities in the world, Mexico City. Autonomous neighborhoods, organized by the direct participation of their inhabitants, and through explicitly politicized movements, have developed into concrete examples of a different form of social organization based on equality and sharing. Space, territory, plays a crucial role, not only in giving ground to those collective experiences but also in shaping them. Such neighborhoods depart from dominant organizational forms of social relations but also explicitly challenge the prevailing characteristics of urban order and urban governance policies meant to sustain it.

One such neighborhood on the eastern outskirts of the enormous metropolitan agglomeration of Mexico City is located in the Acapatzingo area. The neighborhood is often referred to as La Polvorilla. It is part of an initiative by a movement called Los Panchos, which has already established a network of about ten similar neighborhoods in Mexico City (Velázquez 2014: 103). La Polvorilla already has about 3,000 people involved in its development.

"In 1995, Cooperativa Acapatzingo, encompassing 596 families of informally employed people purchased in instalments an abandoned mine used as a rubble depot to build their homes on the premises" (UN Habitat 2004). The value of land was very low and the area was situated at the periphery of the city amid an amorphous urban sprawl characterized by lack of urban installations and very poor housing conditions. Being a politically oriented initiative based on collective self-management and solidarity, the Cooperativa struggled to stay on the land by establishing an informal camp on the site and kept on demanding the economic support of the local and state urban authorities. Local politicians don't dare to create conflicts that they can't control. So, the Cooperativa finally gained access to a collective loan from the state's *Instituto de Vivienda del Distrito Federal* (Zibechi 2014: 55), a public sector institution established by the Mexican Constitution, which

7.1 A part of La Polvorilla neighborhood

explicitly refers to the right to housing. This loan was based on a 30-year credit and was meant to be used for the full payment of the land and the design and construction of the housing settlement.

They call this a project of autonomy; in organizing their own community, people manage to create their own spaces, their own forms of publicness. They are working towards energy self-sufficiency by placing solar panels in common spaces. They don't pay for water, but have installed a common water purification installation. They have their own community gardens, a community radio station, and other shared infrastructure. They don't allow the police to enter, but maintain their own justice system – to create conditions of conviviality based on equality. This is an attempt to create a form of social organization independent of the state, free from state surveillance and control. However, they do this not to isolate themselves in an enclave of other-ness. Cooperativa Acapatzingo is part of a network of similar initiatives, which advance the political effort of Los Panchos to construct popular power while fighting today for a better life in a huge capitalist metropolis.

The second example in Mexico City is also a self-managed neighborhood, created by the *Brújula Roja* (meaning Red Compass) movement. This neighborhood is generally based on the Zapatista values and modes of establishing self-governance – the main streets are named after the most important demands and principles of the Zapatista movement, *Democracia, Dignidad, Educación, Información, Salud* etc. Its name, Tlanezi Calli, in the indigenous language of nahuatl, means 'House of the Dawn'. The approximately 1,150 people in this neighborhood practice urban autonomy in relation to everyday needs for food, healthcare, education, and work in community projects, for instance the construction of an autonomous sewage system. They even have a workshop to make their own clothes.

As both Esteva and Zibechi (among many Latin American thinkers) insist, Latin American anti-systemic movements are very much focused on the control, appropriation, and transformation

7.2 Names of streets in a plan of Tlanezi Calli: a true manifesto

of urban (and rural) territory. It is through the emergence of "territories in resistance" (Zibechi 2012) that those "from below" manage to effectively organize practices and forms of everyday-ness that shape and promote resistance to dominant life-models. Autonomous neighborhoods are such territories of resistance, and, as in every case in the history of dissident mobilizations, their spaces become not only safe shelters for those who struggle against every-day exploitation, misery, and repression but also one of the most necessary means through which new subjects of action emerge.

As Gerardo, an Acpatzingo activist, explains:

> We have decided to create not only housing projects but also com-munities. For us to create a community means to be able to control our territory, to be able to establish our chosen habits and rules and our ways of solving the problems of living together, and thus, to be able to create our own history. Our own process of constructing autonomy.
>
> We have decided to move from the project of creating digni-fied housing conditions to the project of creating a dignified life. This means that we have decided to improve life conditions in our communities by ensuring health, justice, and security, as well as a different work logic for all by reconstructing the social fabric (*tejido social*) which is destroyed. The logic of the system is to progress as individuals competing against others. The principles in our organization emerge naturally, following a respect for others no matter what color their skin or what language they speak. What we all have in common is that they are fucking us, that we are poor. (Gerardo interview)

A crucial defining aspect of these autonomous urban commu-nities is that their cohesion is not based on pre-existing and long established shared identities as is the case of indigenous com-munities. Clarifying this difference Gerardo says:

> Here we belong to different cultures. But we all meet in every-day praxis. Voluntary or community work is something common in indigenous communities. But in cities, too, a similar tradition exists, so comrades are used to it. Instead of allowing a culture to dominate all the others we combine them: for example in common feasts many different cultures coexist (mainly of those who come from south Mexico). This is how to create a shared culture; we

don't think any culture represents absolute truth. Knowledge is produced collectively and through combinations and synthesis. The feeling of belonging to a community is deeply rooted. (Gerardo interview).

Zibechi, too, refers to the "communitarian nature of Mexican *colonias* [urban housing areas]" (Zibechi 2014: 57). From this value system a counter-dominant approach to cultural difference and individual particularity springs. This may be clearly shown in the ways such communities deal with pressing everyday social problems:

> We are part of the society so we have difficulties with intra-family violence, addictions, everything. The difference is in how we deal with these problems. It would be very simple when we identify someone as an alcoholic or drug addict to expel him from our communities but we would not then differ from what the system does to us: the system does not want us because we dress in a certain way or speak in a certain way, it does not want us because we are poor. We don't intend or want to reproduce this logic of the system. What we try to do, in direct confrontation with this logic, is to create our own forms [of living together]. (Gerardo interview)

Accommodating otherness, then, is an essential constituent of autonomous neighborhoods' commoning culture. A shared experience of being the potential (or, often, actual) outcasts of the system unites those people but also teaches them. This is not a struggle of brave and "uncontaminated" idealists. "We are not pure" say the Zapatistas (Esteva 2015: 90). "All of us are crippled – some physically, some mentally, some emotionally" (Illich et al. in Esteva, 2015). Realizing that striving to create a different community does not immediately release you from the devastating behavior control imposed by dominant rules and values is an important lesson being learned collectively in these neighborhoods. So, space and community rules are always developed in a process of expanding the emancipating potentialities of commoning and self-management.

In Acapatzingo, community space production and maintenance are highly indicative of an ongoing struggle to create shared spaces which, however, host the differentiated needs of different inhabitant groups. Grouped around nine open squares with trees and ample open space, houses form smaller neighborhoods of 20–30 individual two-story units. The square for the elderly is different from the square for the young people but both offer opportunities for mixed uses and creative encounters.

Street pavements, in which rich everyday socialization experiences unfold (including inventive children's play) are wide and safe. The main street, named Pancho Villa after the leader of the Mexican Revolution (who is the central inspiring figure for Los Panchos), is a friendly outdoor space with only a few cars passing, and at very low speed. A community garden not only develops with the aim of establishing food sovereignty for the neighborhood but also gives opportunities for collective creative work and for cultivating a different approach to nature: "One of the main objectives of our urban agriculture commission is [to promote] the rescue of the earth, the love of the earth ... I don't know how it is in Greece, but here when we ask a child where does the food come from, they will answer from the market or from Walmart

7.3 La Polvorilla's general assembly meeting place (as well as a soccer field)

7.4 One of La Polvorilla's squares

7.5 Part of La Polvorilla's urban garden

[American supermarket chain]. We have lost our rural origins, our farming descent" (Gerardo interview).

Observing architectural elements which usually regulate a clear and decisively marked transition from outside public space to inside private space, one can recognize in autonomous neighborhoods an effort to shape different spatial relations based on different levels and forms of sharing. Thus, in Acapatzingo the outside is truly common space while the inside, although family space (including spaces of family privacy), is also part of a chain of spaces that characterizes house groups which have a distinct color so as to indicate that they belong to the same group of collective work, a *brigada*. Small family courtyards, which are used especially by the women in their everyday housework, are separated from outside space by a perforated wall. This kind of outside border, a choice made by the general assembly, becomes an active threshold, which both ensures and expresses in architectural form the precarious and precious connection of family life to outdoor activities (both common and "private"). Pursuing similar aims, the El Molino autonomous neighborhood assembly decided to plan and construct houses that have kitchens located at the front of the house so that mothers can see the children playing outside (Zibechi 2014: 52). It was the women's knowledge and active participation in the planning assemblies that provided such crucial insights to the design of the settlements (Gerardo interview). Juarez-Galeana explicitly refers to a relevant participatory planning workshop which took place in La Polvorilla (2006: 192)

In Tlanezi Calli, in front of each house's central door there is a threshold space, a small courtyard which is open but also clearly marked as distinct from the pedestrian streets that shape the settlement's circulation network (no cars are allowed in this housing area). This space becomes an expression of family identity: each household has different ways to project such a shared collective identity (flower pots, decorative elements, mundane objects indicating everyday habits etc.), although this may not always be the result of a conscious "popular design" choice. The fact that those entrances are organized in pairs by the overall plan creates interesting juxtapositions and comparisons. A window opening, which enhances visual communication between those who enter or exit, connects those adjacent threshold areas, giving neighboring families the opportunity to further develop or regulate the sharing of space.

Autonomous metastatic communities?

Autonomous neighborhoods constitute experiments in community organization, collective efforts to create shared worlds in which the urban poor organize to protect themselves from the devastating exploitation conditions that prevail in the city. It is important to understand how those shared worlds are being shaped through practices of collaboration and rules that establish equality. And it is the community as a generator and protector of these shared worlds that defines both the relevant practices and the spaces to house and promote them.

> The prime essence (*instancia superior*) of our communities is the general assembly (every week, every 15 days or every month depending on the rules of the corresponding neighborhood), then the everyday work, which is realized through seven different commissions of our organization: the economic commission, the maintenance commission (responsible for the water and electricity supply as well as for square and garden management), the vigilance commission (which guards our community –police are not allowed to enter – and which solves "social situations" that arise in our community), ... the education and culture commission, ... the communication commission (also responsible for our community radio station), ... the urban agriculture commission and the health commission (including volunteers for health services – *promotores de salud*). (Gerardo interview)

The social organization of the autonomous community, then, is deeply rooted in a collective care for the goods and services which are considered as common. These are to be shared equally, with extra attention for those members who are in most need. Community, thus, is not focused on a technical resource management but develops, instead, a participative form of government which encourages solidarity and builds popular power "from below." A constituent part of this model is the creation of everyday social bonds through organized groups of collaboration.

"In our communities we are organized in brigades. Each brigade has 20–25 people and 7 of them are responsible for connecting the brigade with each one of the seven community commissions" (Gerardo interview). Members of the brigade alternate in various duties and, through this procedure, they not only share the burdens of everydayness but also learn how to do useful things for themselves and for the community (like how to organize a radio program, or how to make a blanket, or maintain a garden). As already mentioned, the houses of those who belong to the same brigade have the same color, which is different from the color of the others.

In Acapatzingo autonomous neighborhood the inhabitants' community established different shared spaces, which can be considered as communal spaces but also as common spaces. This distinction becomes crucial if we aim to trace the commoning potentialities which grow in such socio-spatial arrangements.

Within the perimeter of the neighborhood, shared spaces are spaces of public use predominately for the members of the community. Those include streets, squares, open meeting spaces in which assemblies may take palace (including a football field), urban gardens, and community facilities areas (a water tank, a community radio office, a preparatory school, and a pharmacy). We can call those spaces communal spaces, recognizing that commoning practices develop in them under rules established by the community assembly. Community members may use those spaces and are also responsible for their construction, maintenance, and protection. Commoning is especially limited to community members who participate equally in the various commoning practices. However, as Enrique Reynoso, an Acapatzingo activist, explains in an interview with Raul Zibechi, "We are seeking a utopia that is not an island, but rather an open space that can have a contagious effect on society" (Zibechi 2014: 58). The Acapatzingo community establishes multiple links with its surrounding neighborhoods, "training them in the creation of base-level committees and community security; they also provide advice about how to respond to evictions, which recipients repay in food" (Zibechi, 2014: 58).

Following a similar path of osmotic relations with their urban surrounding, Tlanezi Calli has developed a community center which is located at the perimeter of the neighborhood and has its own distinct entrance. Neighbors and people in need may enter the building and ask for help and support by the community's services (including a pharmacy, a common kitchen, a small preparatory class for school students etc.). This center in more like an osmotic urban threshold, which separates but also connects the heart of the autonomous neighborhood with the nearby urban housing areas.

We can guess, then, that in their contagious relations with the rest of the city, autonomous communities actually develop practices of expanding commoning (Stavrides 2016). People from outside the neighborhood are not simply allowed to use certain of the community facilities (the preparatory school, the pharmacy, or the community building during organized open feasts) but they are invited to be part of a process that attempts to metastasize throughout the city. Can we not, then, consider the corresponding communal spaces as common spaces (Stavrides

7.6 Tlanezi Calli's central square

2016) in the making? Can we not see such spaces as potential catalysts in a commoning chain reaction?

Explicitly referring to the prospect of transplanting the urban commoning momentum developed in autonomous neighborhoods to other urban self-management efforts, Enrique Reynoso, says in another interview: "Rather than grow the scale of our assemblies, we want the assemblies to multiply in other places, in whatever ways are appropriate" (Barrington-Bush 2016).

Autonomous neighborhoods actually participate actively in the promotion of collective resistance initiatives by becoming part of urban struggles, of campaigns, and of movement networks. As Sergio, a member of Tlanezi Calli, remembers, the neighborhood actively mobilized in support of the major struggle of Atenco farmers in 2006 when the neighborhood was at the first phase of its construction. Atenco farmers were clashing with state forces at that time in an effort to keep their flower-growing lands against a devastating compulsory expropriation order issued by the Mexican state in order to promote a pharaonic construction project connected to the development of the city's airport. The Tlanezi people decided to block those streets near their neighborhood which were to be used by police to attack the Atenco movement. Of course, they too had to face the attack of the police riot squads because of their resistance but they have managed to make it substantially more difficult for the harsh suppression of the struggle to become effective (Sergio interview). Blocking the suppressive mechanisms of the state is as much part of the community's struggle for a more just society as is its members' efforts to organize alternative forms of living together, of sharing a common world in the making.

A shared territory

The definition of a shared territory became crucial for the autonomous urban communities of Tlanezi Calli and Acapatzingo. Observing the forms through which this definition is materialized, one may further understand the ways those communities are connected to their territories.

Obviously a gate explicitly marks an "inside" and an "outside."

And, of course, this impression is enhanced by the presence of guardians. A gate regulates and controls a passage. We can, then, talk about an explicitly circumscribed territory, belonging to a community which is determined to keep it and protect it from tresspassers. In both neighborhoods, there exist explicit gates guarded by the inhabitants. In Acapatzingo, gates are marked by a recognizable symbol: a big red star denotes the community's shared ideology. Are we witnessing the presence of a gated community, albeit a collectively created one?

Actually, things are more complicated than they may seem. To understand the conditions of such an urban territory definition we must connect it – and compare it – to another peculiar case of autonomous territory definition, that of the Zapatista *municipios*. One often observes in the Zapatista areas a sign that declares: "*Esta usted en territorio Zapatista en rebeldia. Aqui manda el pueblo y el gobierno obedece*" ("You are in Zapatista territory in rebellion. Here the people dictate and the government obeys"). What, however, is the exact meaning of this "here"? Where exactly is this area? Does it have clearly demarcated borders? Usually, if not always, it doesn't. Villages in the *municipios* may have inhabitants that are not supporters of Zapatistas. And Zapatista *territorios* are scattered in a vast area, in Chiapas, with lots of non-Zapatista villages in-between. The meaning and status quo of the Zapatista area is not based, then, on the existence of a strict borderline that separates it from the rest of the country. In an ongoing contestation with state and paramilitary forces, Zapatista territory is being defined through use and appropriation. Zapatistas have reclaimed vast areas for cultivation which used to belong to local feudal lords. State defined property limits were and keep on being challenged. And there is a constant pressure from the government to re-establish in the area the rules and regulations of the state. So, Zapatista territory is a way of collectively defining through use and through community-decided rules a kind of shared space. Space commoning is based on practices of space appropriation rather than on community guarded borderlines.

Compared to such a process of defining community space, the gate that clearly marks the area of administration buildings of the so-called Juntas de Buen Gobierno in Oventic seems to belong to a different spatial logic. In this case the "here" seems to be clearly marked. However, one can observe that the area has actually rather vague and unprotected limits once one walks away from the buildings and immerses oneself in the surrounding rainforest. Is it, then, that this gate was not meant exactly to control access to the area but was rather constructed as an emblematic structure that tries to express the stark socio-political difference which this form of government explicitly establishes with dominant forms of governance? Is this gate, which hardly defines a closed limited territory, a declaration of difference rather than the imposition of a separation?

Returning to Tlanezi and Acapatzingo, to those autonomous urban areas explicitly influenced by the Zapatista project of autonomy, one can observe similar characteristics in the definition of shared space. True, the conditions in a city, and especially in a huge and differentiated city as the city of Mexico, are quite different from the Chiapas *altos* and the Lacandona rain forest villages. Defining space in a city is always an act that has to do with strict property regulations. However, people in the reclaimed land of those autonomous neighborhoods do not aspire to create their "own" safe havens in the middle of highly dangerous urban *periferias*. They rather attempt to construct shared housing areas to live in, which may be considered as materialized examples of a different kind of urban cohabitation. So their gates do not only try to keep out the threats that come from state or paramilitary forces. This attempt, anyhow, would be as meaningless as it is to barricade an autonomous area in Lacandona. Military or paramilitary forces can't be warded off by the efficiency of gates or borderline constructions but may only be countered by efficient community mobilizations and solidarity networks. So these neighborhood gates are more like declarations of autonomy, the way the Oventic gate is. It is not by chance that in Acapatzingo the emblems of the community's values are on the gates to express a meaningful difference. And, of course, in spite of the everyday mundane rituals of gate crossing, those who would want to enter with malignant intentions could almost effortlessly do so from less guarded areas that surround both neighborhoods.

The fact of controlling a gate through the everyday presence of

community members, who rotate in this duty, creates a ceremoni-
ously established feeling of belonging to an autonomous territory.
To understand this it would suffice to observe the determination
and even perhaps pride radiating from an old woman standing as

7.7 Guarding a symbolic gate with the determination only a commoning
project can support!

a guard at one of the gates of Acapatzingo. She is surely defending something which is more than a territory. She is protecting a way of life which is in stark contrast to the surrounding poor and drug-governed neighborhood.

Maybe there is a lesson to be learned here. Space commoning as a crucial aspect of urban autonomy is not necessarily connected to a spatially defined community sovereignty or to the protection of a common property. Space commoning may radiate as a counter-example through territorial relations that are more complex. These relations are being performed in explicit acts of self-governance by and through commoning. And they may be understood only in the context of networks of cooperation and solidarity. Zapatista communities draw their power to exist from the relations of cooperation and mutual support between villages as regulated by the Juntas de Buen Gobierno. And the autonomous urban communities are equally able to establish their presence in the city because they proliferate through networks of mutual help and expanding empowerment. Their strength, symbolically expressed in their gates, is really dependent upon those expanding networks. And one of their more powerful means to protect themselves and to flourish is to disconnect the collective imaginary of their inhabitants from the image of a closed growing enclave of otherness.

They are different and they know it. But they struggle to make this difference important for the lives of those who share with them the same problems of mass expulsion: the urban poor.

The gate considered as an architectural element that shapes spatial relations may seem to be necessarily connected to the definition of controlled passages. However, the experience of the autonomous communities shows that gates can be not only organizational architectural forms but, importantly, expressive elements of a different understanding of territory. A recognizable architectural form, in such a context, becomes the concrete expressive materialization of the values connected to the shared spaces it gives access to. Throughout history, gates have been connected to dominating values ceremonially expressed. Let us not forget that the triumphal arcs, erected as memorials of an emperor's successful war, were initially only temporary constructions, which had the form of gates through which the victorious leader entered the city. So, to reshape the meaning of gates in autonomous Mexican neighborhoods is part of a process of redefining the public uses and meanings of shared space as common space.

Autonomous neighborhoods in Mexico City directly challenge the dominant rules of urban governance. Producing in action elements of a popular self-management, they indeed shape a form of social organization in which commoning rather than capitalist command becomes the predominant characteristic.

As seen, commoning in such neighborhoods is not simply a set of sharing practices that assists the urban poor to survive in precarious urban communities, although its importance in collective urban survival is of utmost importance. Commoning becomes the propelling force for the building of different, counter-dominant relations of collaboration and decision-making. Urban self-management as a specific counter-dominant model of urban governance emerges through a set of practices and collective rule

7.8 Commoning work while constructing the neighborhood

making decisions that establish what participants themselves call autonomy (*autonomias* – in the plural).

Autonomy as a project and as unfolding collective experience does not develop, however, in the form of self-sustained and bar-ricaded enclaves of "otherness." It is a metastatic virus-like form of social organization, which attempts to establish networks of urban resistance in the process of building potentially emancipa-tive relations of cohabitation. The prefigurative and exemplary elements of these urban practices are firmly based on experiences that people-in-need develop in their struggle for a decent life. Autonomous neighborhoods, thus, may be at times tolerated by the dominant urban order, since they appear as a lesser evil compared to the possibility of urban unrest caused by desper-ate populations. However, they are actually a constant threat to dominant urban governance since they constitute organized shelters for the "dangerous classes." Choosing not to be satisfied by their small safe havens in the midst of an urban archipelago of violent clashes and rigid power geometries based on exploitation and segregation, autonomous neighborhoods actively politicize their existence. They become condensers, catalysts, and often igniters of urban struggles. And they show in practice that a dif-ferent form of urban governance based on sharing, equality, and solidarity is not only possible but also urgently needed. Against the highly discriminatory policies of the Mexican state, which is increasingly becoming the arena of rivaling elites, and against the local mafias (connected in various ways with the economic and political elite), which impose harsh rules in the neighborhoods of the poor, *autonomias* build a structure of self-government based on the sharing of power. If urban commoning may acquire the power to challenge capitalist urban governance it will be through such organized struggles for building metastatic shared worlds, in and against the dominant urban order.

8

Objects in common: objects for commoning

The IMPA challenge

We have already encountered and explored the potentialities of shared spaces in some exemplary cases of collective housing. We have seen how the question of mass production housing does not have to be answered by proposals resulting in uniformity and presupposing social homogenization. One of the points of this book is to support the idea that commoning, either during the production of spaces to be shared or in the actual sharing of spaces in the process of cohabitation, should not be based on the abolishing of differences, in form as well as in practices. Commoning, and space commoning in particular, develops through negotiations between equals and integrates differences as long as the common space of sharing is recognized.

In this chapter the problem of how to develop and sustain the production of common spaces, by continuously struggling against the tendency of communities of commoners to enclose themselves, is approached through a different spatiality level: the spatiality of the object. Are objects which appear in inhabiting spaces, or objects which are found in shared spaces, merely useful tools for human relations to unfold or do they become active factors in shaping and expressing those relations? Are arrangements of objects ways of actually giving form to space? And is it in our everyday experiences that we use such objects to actively transform, facilitate, and expand practices of sharing? Furthermore, since we live in a period in which most of these objects are standardized and mass produced, how can the quest for individualization within commoning develop, use, or re-interpret those objects?

Such questions will be explored through the careful analysis of an art project: a strange choice, indeed, since we know that art objects are really quite distinct and usually separated from the realm of mundane everydayness. However, an artistic practice involving a performative interpretation of an everyday mundane object, a chair, may possibly expose the power to potentialize space hidden in the production and use of such an object. Can we see a chair, or many identical chairs, as mediators of sharing and, more than that, carriers of an open community of commoners in the making? The project "Sitting is a Verb" seems to hint towards such a possibility.

This project took place at IMPA, a so-called "recuperated factory" (*empresa recuperada*) in Buenos Aires from December 2010 to January 2011. A visual artist, Aimée Zito Lema, and a social anthropologist, Nahuel Blaton, conceived this project as an artistic contribution to a larger project: the creation of a University of Workers inside the IMPA building complex.

IMPA has a pioneering role in the movement of factory occupations which swept Argentina, especially during and after the 2001 crisis (Vieta 2014, Ruggeri and Vieta 2015). IMPA has been a worker-managed factory since 1998, when the workers decided to take their work in their hands as the enterprise was almost bankrupt and they were left without jobs. From then on, they organized a production process that was able to support their lives, specializing in aluminum products (IMPA was actu-ally an aluminum plant). But they soon realized that they could not survive as a self-managed production place without the active support and participation of people from the neighbor-hood (IMPA is located in the centrally situated neighborhood Almagro) and the movements.

This would be a necessary addition to IMPA workers' active involvement in acts of solidarity to workplace occupation move-ments, as, for example, in the case of Chilavert graphic arts: "The IMPA assembly ... defended the factory by standing in front of it, linking arms to make a chain" (Sitrin 2006: 70). So they started to

8.1 IMPA recuperated factory

create inside the remaining vast and disused areas of IMPA what they called a Cultural City Factory. Soon this cultural and social center included a secondary school specializing in cooperative education, a school for adult learning, a radio and TV station, rehearsal and performance spaces, and an ambitious popular university program called University of the Workers. Extracts from a relevant Declaration of Principles are indicative of this project's ambition to establish an alternative University:

> We call people to unite in establishing a University of the Workers, moved by the desire to make this an effective tool in a struggle that remains just and necessary …

> We strive for an education in which knowledge is jointly constituted by all and in which everyone gives the best of him- or herself from his or her own experience …

> The critical consciousness of the workers must grow with the right to the appropriation of, and compliance with, all the knowledge of a society that runs on the workers' enormous effort …

A challenge awaits us. (Buenos Aires 2010, included in the exhibition catalogue: Zito Lema and Blaton 2012)

This University already has an interesting and inspiring history. During the first stage of its establishment, however, important needs had to be satisfied. One of them: chairs for the future students.

Not just any chair

The project "Sitting is a Verb – Rietveld for IMPA" was conceived as an effort to provide IMPA's new University with 100 chairs. However, this was not simply a gesture of support aimed at providing what was urgently needed. As Zito Lema and Blaton specify: "Not just any old chairs, but chairs whose design and concept fit the ideals for which the University of Workers stands" (2012: 5). This is why they decided to create, through this project, chairs according to a design model introduced by Geritt Rietveld, a Dutch pioneer modernist designer, whose approach to mass-production design was connected to values of knowledge sharing and active involvement of the users.

Named "crate chair," this chair model was developed by Rietveld in 1934. It actually belonged to a series of experimental models he devised in an effort to make available cheap, affordable, and easy to assemble objects for home use. The series initially included an armchair, a low table, and a book case and was later further expanded with a crate desk, another low table, and an upright chair (Van Zijl and Kuper 1992: 155).

Crate furniture in general and crate chair specifically were designed according to the idea that people themselves could readily assemble them using planks cut in appropriate sizes that were joined together with tongue-and-groove screws. Planks would be easily mass produced and thus the chair itself would be rather cheap, since assembling work was transferred to the user. As we learn from a response by Rietveld to a really crushing criticism published in *Bouwkunding Wekblad* (October 1935), he aimed at simplicity and for the unadorned appearance of the chair. He even advised that chairs would better remain unpainted or, alternatively, users should paint each plank separately so that after screwing them together "joints or screws are not hidden away" (Van Zijl and Kuper 1992: 155; also Máčel et al. 2008: 217). Actually, after being accused of falling "below every professional standard" in the above critique, he responded that the proposed construction method "goes straight to its goal ... unsullied by the working frowns of our craftsmen" (Máčel et al. 2008: 217).

It seems that for Rietveld, craft furniture combined ideas related to mass affordability and mass production as well as ideas about construction simplicity with an emphasis on rational, clearly expressed, and visible joints. Construction itself was not under-stood as a purely mechanical process. We know that Rietveld cared about the way workers were involved in the production process (he hoped to ease their burden through design choices) and that he advocated for design solutions that implicitly or explicitly opted for collaboration practices. In a striking remark, based on Rietveld's writings, Michael White informs us that the word for joints that he uses in Dutch, "*verbinding* (joining) carries connotations both of conjunction and union, as well as com-munication and combination (especially of colours)" (2003: 2) According to the same author, Rietveld's famous crossing joint, where elements extend past the point of junction, "allowed each structural element to preserve a separate visual identity while clearly expressing its dependency on its neighbours" (2003: 2). The same expressivity of joints and the corresponding ethic of "collaboration" seem to be present in crate furniture: parts are clearly separated but are meant to depict an organization that expresses its unity. Besides, the notion of collaboration (*samen-werking*) was, as White suggests, a central notion for the De Stijl, the aesthetic movement in which Rietveld actively participated (2003: 2). In the first De Stijl manifesto (1918) we read that the new artists are fighting "against the domination of individual despotism. They therefore sympathize with all, who work for the formation of an international unity of life."

Rietveld may not have explicitly declared that his crate furniture was a response to the prevailing economic crisis of the 1930s. His approach to social problems, and to the values of collaboration, were rather embedded on his design efforts and on his longing of a democratically shared craftsmanship. His belief in mass production was connected to mass affordability and his design ideas actually preceded the DIY culture by establishing its value on collaboration and participation rather than on individualism. Zito Lema comments on Rietveld's social awareness by considering him a kind of socialist (Zito Lema interview). His social involvement was indeed reflected in his lectures as a teacher. "It's a much better task to design a glass that many people can drink from than one beautiful crystal glass, attainable for only the very few" (quoted by Ida Van Zijl in Zito Lema and Blaton 2012: 10).

Chairs in common

The art project Rietveld for IMPA was an attempt to activate the potentialities of a chair model in support of a multileveled commoning experience. This was not only a way to support a University that was being established as a commoning procedure within an occupied workplace made productive through sharing and cooperation. The project tried to orient the means through which its contribution to the emerging University was realized towards a commoning ethos. The chair chosen contained in the logic of its design and production a value system which is very close to commoning: Rietveld was, of course, not exactly an advocate of commoning but his ideas, as it is hopefully made apparent so far, were part of a perhaps utopian attempt to think of mass production as an opportunity for the democratic sharing of products, knowledge, and practices of creation. In Zito Lema's interpretation, crate chair was not simply a mass production object but, crucially, an object designed to foster "an equality of possibilities" (Zito Lema interview).

One step further in activating the potential of the crate chair is to shape its production through voluntary participation, and since this was meant to be not only a practical task (to make these 100 chairs needed) but also an artistic gesture, Zito Lema and Blaton paid careful attention to the elements of expressiveness and symbolization. Thus, going beyond a mere execution of the collective crate chair construction they composed an emphatic ode to commoning as a community creating power.

As Zito Lema remarks: "There is something that happens when people engage physically with labor" (interview). This something for her was located both in an awareness of the effort needed to produce in common (including the awareness of bodies being in coordination and collaboration) and in the experience of an emerging community of commoners. More than 80 people – students, artists, activists, as well as neighbors and some of the IMPA workers – participated in the collective effort to construct the chairs. Interestingly, after the chairs were completed, they "placed a small metal plate (produced at the IMPA factory) bearing the name of the contributor/creator on every seat" (Zito Lema and Blaton, 2012: 6). Since the materials for the chairs were bought with money collected through crowd funding, this is a gesture of including both those "who donated labor and those who donated money" (Zito Lema interview) in this collective endeavor.

This commoning community was established through collective work and by sharing an ethics of the gift. But it was not a community of philanthropists. By participating in the project people actually became coexplorers of the potentialities of commoning. As Horacio González observes in relation to the future students of the University who participated in the project: "what a student

8.2 Collaborating to produce the Rietveld chairs in IMPA

learns and writes by means of his chair is partially the knowledge he has attained by actually making the thing. 'Owning one's own experience' could be the slogan of the Worker's University" (Zito Lema and Blaton, 2012: 7).

This was, therefore, a project of really potentializing a space of alternative education by literally re-creating an object which could epitomize in its design, in its production, and in its use a promise of sharing. Interestingly, the project raises important issues connected to the values and practices of sharing between equals. Does sharing diminish differences? Not really, each one of the participants left his or her mark on the chair – a small tablet with a name. Individual contributions are recorded but on an equalizing basis.

Does sharing necessarily need to refer to equal amounts of something or identical objects for everyone? To this the artist seems to have a clear view: "For me it was important that the chairs were supposed to be all the same. I think it is better to have the chairs in their original generalness and abstractness" (Zito Lema interview). Some wanted to paint "their" chairs or to decorate them – indeed a resurfacing of a will to differentiation (if not distinction) that may be connected to the distinctive character of an art object. Such objects are presented as unique even when they are produced as multiple: various forms of authentication are devised in order to disconnect them from the "vulgarity" of mass production, the creator's signature included. To learn to produce a "lightly," so to speak, individualized object (meant to be used as a generic object that nevertheless carries with it the memory of the individuals who produce it) is a lesson in commoning that carefully balances individual contributions (and needs) with the prospect of community building. A cooperative University is, after all, a project that promotes individual learning through sharing and collaboration by devising the means of sharing and the knowledge to be shared.

What kind of potential space emerged through the practices of commoning triggered by this project? If we employ the three-fold distinction suggested in chapter 2, which tries to locate the potentialities of architectural form, we may discover three differing (albeit overlapping) ways of potentializing space through the Rietveld for IMPA project:

1. The chair as generator of spatial arrangements which enhance commoning (the organizational aspect of form).
2. The chair as medium of expression of shared values (connected to community making and to participatory education).
3. The chair as an object produced through collaboration employing materials and technology accessible to all.

Let us explore these three ways one by one:

When Zito Lema was asked why she didn't prefer to use a kind of seating object that encourages people to sit together, as for example happens in the use of the bench, she replied that the very form of seating arrangement preferred by the University students is seating in a circle. "Classes happen usually in circles" (Zito Lema interview).

Interestingly, crate chairs were first produced as "weekend furniture" by the company Metz En Co in 1935. A relaxed atmosphere, a simple chair, seemingly designed to withstand harsh weather and casual use without any pretension of monumentality. Rational design was one of Rietveld's scopes and surely this chair is very closely connected to this scope. However, transferring this object to a context so remote from weekend family scenes creates new possible object arrangements. From a set of objects similar in style that were supposed to participate in an arrangement of leisure to a series of identical chairs organized to form a class: the crate chair becomes an active element in the arrangement of bodies in collaboration (in the context of alternative education). Distinct individual presences become integrated in a learning community which is comprised of different people with a common scope. A community of singularities sitting in identical chairs arranged in ways which reflect both the common scope and the means to reach it. And this is not an arrangement of comfortable chairs, let us note. Their design is not based on the use of soft materials and does not aim at supporting highly relaxed body postures: an austere chair, unadorned and cheap, is used to create a class arrangement based on an economizing ethics that rejects pretention. Students thus will become aware, through bodily experience too, that what they participate in is characterized by the processing of individual experiences and knowledges through a sharing economy of means.

There is a certain awkward feeling in seeing the crate chairs arranged in rows or in circles. Our inherited appreciation of modernist furniture design is firmly grounded on the admiration of unique objects. Objects that were conceived as basically functional and essentially mass produced have now become emblematically unique art objects. This is a real reversion of the modernist design ethos Zito Lema says (interview). So returning the chair to a status of the "multiple," giving it the identity of a module to be used in arrangements, makes it again an object-catalyst of shared and similar experiences. A possible rediscovering of the crate chair through a commoning education?

Commoning collaboration: art, work, or play?

Were the Rietveld chairs produced for the IMPA University art objects? Was this an artistic project? Zito Lema defines it "as an artistic project in a social context," and adds: "My questions for conceiving this project were also artistic" because "a question and a gesture are as important as having the object at the end" (interview).

What makes chair production an artistic project is obviously not that the final products (the chairs) were considered as artwork. The process of the chair-making was already a performance piece which could be considered as artistic. However, this was not an explicitly staged event for others to see, to experience, and perhaps to contemplate upon. What converted a mere act of plan-execution and manual work into a performance was the scope of this act to express values meant to be activated in an emerging alternative education setting. Acting in concert was meant to symbolize and even prefigure learning in concert. So, commoning was implicitly the content of this artistic performance: we construct chairs together to show that we need to construct learning and knowledge together.

However, the process of making the chairs is also presenting through its forms of actions what is to be understood as commoning if this understanding it is to be experienced through the body.

8.3 Presenting the project inside IMPA where the University of Workers is situated

Means (of presenting the value of commoning) look like the ends (commoning as collaboration of equals).

These remarks, as obvious as they may seem, do have important consequences in rethinking art through commoning. Beyond the distinction between a useful object and an art object (considered as an object of no use), the Rietveld-IMPA chairs were artworks by being useful (as functional) but also by being emblems of cooperation, symbolic condensations of an emerging autonomous education spirit.

Compared to the works of the aesthetic regime of art as defined by Rancière, these are really performed objects, objects that both represent and "work," objects that are meant to recite again and again their history as markers of a value system. According to Rancière, "The art of the aesthetic age has never stopped playing on the possibility that each medium could offer to blend its effects with those of others, to assume their role and thereby create new figures, reawakening sensible possibilities which they had exhausted" (2009: 131–132). This approach does not merely comment upon the mixed media employed in contemporary art.

It suggests that there is a certain "reawakening" which takes place: artistic gestures connected to this new regime of art (actually considered as a re-definition of art whose genealogy Rancière traces back to Winckelman) are supposedly creating new connections between the sensible and the thinkable by questioning the social status of both of them.

It is these connections that characterize the ways contemporary artistic practices explore new forms of life through art by questioning or overtly challenging the borders between life and art. Commenting on the work of Dzinga Vertov, Rancière wants to show how his films actually tried to depict (or rather gesture towards) a new life in-the-making which was made possible in a revolutionary condition. Thus, "a great symphony of movement, a great manifestation of the new collective life innerving all activities" (2017: 615) became possible. But this was not merely a didactic representation of the marvels of organized production under socialism. This was more like a hymn to collective vitality, a hymn to life that was not connected to a specific narrative, to a specific activity, to a specific cause-effect explanation. "The artist wants to show that the practice of art is exactly the same as the practice of industrial life. But this identity is shown by absorbing the ends and means of industrial life within the short circuit of life expressing itself and enhancing itself" (2017: 615).

One can begin to question Rancière's interpretation by observing that the interplay between pure didacticism and experimental explorations in formal language (including abstract geometry in painting or dance and unexpected montage in cinema) was a process of intervention deliberately chosen by artists in face of a revolutionary rethinking of art's social role. This interplay (or conjunction) was not necessarily contradictory: let us not forget that the aspirations for human emancipation were universalizing at those times, the way experimental formal languages were supposed to be. The quest for universal languages united various modernisms in the arts, functionalist aesthetics in architecture included. What, however, one cannot miss is the will to declare, not simply depict or prove, the aim to create an imaginary that transcends existing arrangements of the sensible.

Returning to the IMPA chairs: these are simultaneously utili-

8.4 Chairs inside the factory's Museo IMPA

tarian objects and objects of art. They are the result of a gesture
that fuses life with art by keeping the tension between them alive,
albeit latent.

Parallel to Rancière's analysis one could claim that the IMPA
chair was an object freed from its narrative status (to narrate
its use, to express and thus accommodate sitting) the way the
"renovators of dance and theatre freed bodily movements from
the shackles of a plot" and also "from rational intentional action
directed towards an end" (2013: xv). This would connect the
object chair to the finality of art and disconnect it from the finality
of life. However, what makes these chairs an interesting experiment in art commoning, and in commoning through art, is that
they were meant to be literally used too. They were not meant
to be preserved as exhibits of an artistic declaration (possibly
expressing the values of commoning). Therefore, no suspension
of action, no suspension of plot takes place in the long run. A new
kind of plot is involved that reconfigures action. Collaboration
in the context of this project is both a joyous experience and an

efficient practice. Collaboration is prefigurative (meaning: able to show a possible different future) as well as an experienced challenge to the order of "sensible" practices. Collaboration, thus, becomes an art just because it is part of a life that tries to go beyond existing life patterns. Collaboration is the re-invention of a meaningful plot for an emancipated shared life.

Were the Rietveld-IMPA chairs the product of a de-activation process as described and propagated by Agamben? Let us recall: in his approach, freeing human life from the shackles of capitalism means reclaiming the power-not-to: "it is only in living life that a form-of-life can constitute itself as the inoperativity immanent in every life" (2014: 74). In art (as in politics) it is not that a different kind of work will replace the burden of exploitative labor but a lack of work, a suspension of work, an inactivity which actually de-activates the conditions of exploitation and control.

On a certain level a de-activation of prevalent conditions of capitalist ethos and corresponding governance conditions took place during the "Sitting is a Verb" project. The construction of the chairs was not really a burden but a choice and the emblematic conditions of play characterized the forms of collaboration which were unfolding during the process. If it was merely a performance on stage, of course, this kind of play-like condition would have been identified totally with the project. However, rendering the usual working conditions (and the corresponding ethos) inoperative did indeed produce a work: materialized and tangible, the product of a collective effort. So, play became a different value-context for productive work. However, this was not simply a process of liberating the chair's use-value from its exchange value. It was a form of playing aimed at expressing the value of collaboration by showing, at the same time, that working together may contribute to the development of shared needs and aspirations.

In Rancière's reasoning there is a crucial common ground between the aesthetics of politics and the polities of aesthetics: the reconfiguration of the order of the sensible (2010: 140). The difference, essential as it is, lies in the fact that, whereas in the former this re-configuration happens through the political process of subjectivation which introduces newcomers to the distribution of the sensible, the latter constitutes practices and modes of visibility of art that re-configure the fabric of sensory experience (2010: 140).

In the IMPA chairs project both processes seem to converge: it is the emergence of new subjects of action and enunciation that upsets the order of the sensible which characterizes formal education. A workers' university is truly a chain of political actions that unveils new subjects who demand a role in the definition, production, and sharing of knowledge. The potential subjects of this process are present in the construction of chairs, either literally, or in a projected form, as future users of the chairs.

At the same time, the chairs themselves, having emerged as the product of an artistic project, become bearers of a challenge to the established sensible order: their materiality, as well as their spatial form, along with the possibility of their participation in arrangements that facilitate collaboration in learning, constitute instances of collaboration-through-sharing. They are not merely the result of a collaboration-through-sharing process, they are in a state of continuous potentialization of this process.

Threshold qualities, and, thus, threshold dynamics, may emerge in the arrangements and the production of objects that are being used collectively. As the example of the Rietveld chairs project suggests, through objects crucial relations between people may be formed, challenged, or developed. True, the case examined cannot contain a whole field of research that may reveal the commoning potentialities sparked by the design, production, and use of objects (especially those that seem to connect to mundane "needs" or "functions"). However, within an art project context, the Rietveld chairs became in an emphatic way catalysts of community experiences which may have been temporary but were potentially mentality-shaping. Collaboration is not only a productive activity but also a possible instance of practiced solidarity. This surfaced as knowledge acquired through the collaborating bodies both in the actual crafting labor involved in the chairs' production as well as in the shaping of a shared educational environment.

9

Emancipating commoning?

This book was written in search of emancipatory potentialities in urban commoning practices. The search was focused on both actual contemporary practices and on theorizations that explore ideas and concepts useful for the appraisal of such practices. Out of this project there seems to emerge an interpretative matrix, which also aspires to be suggestive of future actions, based in the interconnections of three terms: the common, community, and space.

Linked to specific social contexts these three terms can indeed support a rethinking of emancipation, considered as a process rather than as a specific final scope.

"Incompletion and provisionality belong to the essence of democracy" says Laclau (1996: 16). But maybe the same phrase can be used, not following Laclau, to describe emancipation. True, as he insists, emancipation presupposes a relation between an oppressor and the oppressed which is formative of both. According to this reasoning there exist no separate identities that can be emancipated, since every "oppressed" identity is the result of a relation and will vanish when the relation is destroyed. If "social agents have to recognize their concrete finitude" (1996: 16) there is no place to claim for a total outside, suitable for all, as a condition of emancipated society.

However, by considering emancipation as a process we can possibly explore this process's characteristics in connection to a reclaiming of the common. Emancipation is, I suggest, a process which potentializes relations of commoning in the direction of equality and solidarity. Providing a rather provisional definition, this suggestion tries to keep open the emancipatory process to different historical trajectories. Furthermore, while it offers criteria for judging the results of this process (does it move towards equality and solidarity?), it doesn't try to preclude the form the process will take. However, this "definition" is not really enough. We need concrete ideas that may connect such a process to the actuality of the contemporary struggles (real existing ones but also potential ones). And for this we need to learn from actually unfolding experiences of emancipation.

Foucault, as we know, has been rather skeptical about the process (or the project) of emancipation. Especially in his late work, he chooses to emphasize "practices of freedom" rather than liberation. And this has direct connection to the distinction between power and domination which is fundamental throughout his work. For him, in a state of domination, "power relations, instead of being mobile, allowing the various participants to adopt strategies modifying them, remain blocked, frozen." In such a state "any reversibility of movement" is blocked by economic, political or military means (1997: 283). Although he explicitly states that his main concern is practices of freedom, he agrees that "[the process of] liberation is sometimes the political or historical condition for a practice of freedom … Liberation paves the way for new power relationships, which must be controlled by practices of freedom" (1997: 283–284).

What if, however, an emancipating society (and not an emancipated society considered as history's end) is a society which gives people the means to exercise practices of freedom, practices, that is, which unblock established geometries of power consolidated in systems of domination? In such a prospect, we need to define the necessary preconditions of these practices rather than prescribe (or canonize) their results. For practices of freedom to be part of a process of social emancipation, they have to contribute, implicitly or explicitly, to the prevention of any accumulation of power. Domination is based precisely on asymmetries in the possession of power. Thus it feeds necessarily from the accumulation of power in the hands of specific groups or members of the society.

I believe that Foucault's understanding of power may help us locate the problem of dealing with power within the prospect of emancipation rather than conceiving power as a threatening outside. If human social relations necessarily involve relations of power and if power may produce (knowledges as well as forms of work and experiences) rather than only destroy (when exercised on those who cannot defend their lives), then what is at stake in an emancipating society is not the elimination of power but the sharing of power, the equal distribution of power between the members of this society. And since power can be linked to economy (including production relations), to education, to political decision-making, and to the production of meaning (in culture, the arts, religion etc.), the equal distribution of power is a very complicated process which will necessarily involve uneven steps in the different historical conjectures in which emancipation unfolds.

Laclau sates that "any theory about power in a democratic society has to be a theory about the forms of power which are compatible with democracy, not about the elimination of power" (1996: 115). In response to this I would suggest that if democracy has any meaning today it is in describing a society that develops towards human emancipation. And that the only power arrangements that promote such a dubious, precarious and not guaranteed development are arrangements that tend towards equality of means to exert power. Because power happens, power is constituted through the historical actualization of social relations (defined as structures of social interaction).

So, the most crucial issue at stake in struggles for emancipation is to limit domination, to share power. In societies in which sharing rather than individual appropriation of vital resources prevails, the form of sharing indicates modes of power sharing. Sharing thus has to do with "technologies of government" that will link the problem of the distribution of resources to the problem of the distribution of power. Put another way, any form of commoning will have to answer the question of power. Is it commoning based on equal access to power or commoning which perpetuates asymmetries of power although certain aspects of social life are based on sharing? We know, for example, that in many societies the family is a hierarchical mini-universe of social relations but the distribution of certain goods may be based on the equal access of all of its members. Also, a group of commoners may function through an established non-hierarchical set of rules as long as it maintains relations of domination with its outside.

In every society the definition and the production of the common is open to antagonism, to polemics (to remember Rancière's emblematic phrase which sees politics as a polemic over the common). If the common is at the center of society's survival and reproduction, there are two parallel processes that regulate the practices which claim and define it. One has to do with conflicting or even contrasting interests. Different groups in society try to establish their particularity as part of this common, or to identify their particularity with the common at stake. The other process has to do with the means that groups of interest have at their disposal, which give them the power to usurp the common, to appropriate it, and to exclude others from this appropriation.

Interestingly, dominant elites more often than not will present themselves as guardians of the common, although they cancel its "commonality." Emancipating commoning tends to exit from both of those processes and so, necessarily, opens new problems in the "technologies of government": what remains of particular interest in this commoning process? How is the danger of unilaterally appropriating the common to be faced in this context?

What the cases explored throughout this book seem to suggest is that the way commoning is linked to emancipatory processes depends on the characteristics of the community that practices it. Expanding commoning is developed by open communities of commoners. Openness, however, does not simply mean lack of rules or lack of spatial indicators that mark this community's common space. Openness is always a space-specific and time-specific characteristic of a community, which actively develops it in an ongoing struggle with forces both within the community and from without, which promote enclosure practices. Openness is a stake to be claimed.

Roberto Esposito offers an interesting suggestion to the problematization concerning the potential openness of community.

The term he introduces, "immunization," aims to describe the
processes through which communities defend themselves from
external threats, but also processes which protect individual
members form the very social bonds that connect them to others.

According to this view, there is an inherent contradiction in
immunitary dynamics: "that which protects the body (the individual body, the social body, and the body politic) is at the same
time that which impedes its development" (2013: 85). The solution
that Esposito suggests is rather vague: immunization is necessary
as long as it does not become overwhelmingly dominant so that it
destroys the common of community. And the bad effects of par-
oxysmic immunization can only be confronted by the expansion
and maintenance of the common (2013: 89). This might entail
"the possibility of a positive, communitarian reconversion of the
… immunitary *dispositif*" (2006: 54; emphasis in original).

At the heart of this approach to the common lies an understanding of the being-together as a form of constitutive sharing.
Putting an emphasis on the etymological root of community,
munus, Esposito claims that community is founded on the obligation to give (2010: 5): *munus* means duty, post, and gift. "What
predominates in the *munus* is … reciprocity or 'mutuality' … of
giving that assigns the one to the other in an obligation" (2010: 6).
Thus, community, "isn't the subject's expansion or multiplication
but its exposure to what interrupts the closing" (2010: 8).

In this approach the common is based neither on the definition
of a common proper (a common identity) nor on the delineation
of a common proper-ty. Community is constituted through the
obligation to exit the individual by recognizing the obligation to
give, to connect to others in offering. And this means sacrificing
one's own enclosure. Whereas *community*, thus, necessarily opens
individuals to others and is sustained through the development of
the common as an open process, *immunity* builds barriers which
divide in order to protect.

Perhaps we need to question the relevance of the immunity
metaphor for the description of society or community. At the
heart of this metaphor is a biological mechanism that is unde-
niably to be considered as a defense mechanism. By using this
knowledge as a substratum of the social immunization metaphor,

one fails to challenge, or at least examine, the condition of the threat. As the case of autoimmune diseases, on which Esposito also comments, shows, the recognition of an enemy is sometimes a false recognition. However, what is lost in this metaphor is the richness of protection strategies developed in different societies. In many cases immunization against an outer threat cannot offer an explanation capable of encompassing the inherent ambiguity of relevant processes. Protection may enter in a relation to what was initially conceived as a threat. In modern child-raising, for example, very often one needs, as a parent or teacher, to redefine threats: one can even recognize benevolent stimuli where others only see threats. In the dynamics of protection, human relations develop in ways that re-define community's (or each individual's) outside. Affective exchanges, probing gestures, and value clashes explicitly shape the field of protection as well as its symbolizations, which actively participate in the redefinition of possible threats.

Although Esposito's direct challenge to our firmly established preoccupations, which consider community as the locus of a shared identity, is crucially important today, the dialectics between the sharing of what is considered as common and the opening of this sharing to others (and to ourselves being transformed by those processes) needs to be further explored. Examining solidarity both as a descriptive term and through its etymological analysis will offer us the means to trace the founding status of this potentiality to open. We know that Durkheim suggested that we need to distinguish between "mechanical solidarity" and "organic solidarity" (2014). The former is based on bonds established and being practiced in traditions which remain unquestionably valid. The latter is based on relations between a society's members developed because different roles and tasks are dependent on one another. Organic solidarity is supported by relations of complementarity, whereas mechanical solidarity is based on relations of similarity. No matter how accurately these forms of solidarity correspond to modern and pre-modern societies respectively, the distinction between them may help in problematizing community as an open rather than as a closed field of commoning.

Tracing the roots of the word solidarity in Latin languages

(which seems a rather new word – probably a creation of the nineteenth century) we find the word solid. By meaning "whole" and "compact as a whole," solid offers to solidarity an image that greatly interferes with the connotations of its use. To be in solidarity might mean to belong to the same solid whole, to be part of a whole that is solid. So, solidarity as a characteristic of community seems to carry with it images of homogeneity and continuity: a kind of crafted unity which presents itself as inseparability.

If, however, we trace the history of the Greek word αλληλεγγύη, which is supposed to correspond to solidarity, at its roots we find a different image. The word seems to have emerged in the Hellenistic period but we encounter its uses during the Byzantine era too. Αλληλεγγύη (from άλληλος meaning each other, and εγγύηση meaning guarantee) corresponds to a situation in which one is being the guarantor of the other. One offers a guarantee for someone in need of it. Interestingly, this word has in its etymology the offer as the condition of building a bond between people.

Returning to the problematization of openness, then, we can possibly see in the dynamic of solidarity (supported by its Greek etymology but also by its current enactments) the potentiality of expanding practices of sharing. Solidarity understood in this way is not simply a bonding practice that creates solid unities but a series of offers which establish interchanges and mutual dependencies. The complementarity connected to the Durkheimian organic solidarity seems to be compatible with such an interpretation of solidarity's dynamics.

Guarantees extend and establish relations. Even in war treaties, and surely in trade negotiations and transactions, established agreements without guarantees are considered as empty. So, openness, we might conclude, is a process of negotiating the common through commoning practices that establish relations between those who participate in those practices. In a way, commoning is both presupposed as an ethics of negotiations but is simultaneously developed and tested by the actual negotiations that unfold in time.

A community which tends towards emancipation is a community that develops a specific form of openness: a regulated and interactive openness. Regulated because no community will ever be sure enough that all external forces are benign and collaborative. And interactive because openness is actually a gesture towards the other and the outer. Openness, thus, welcomes (in ways that may vary of course depending on the historical context), calls upon, and is being activated by the power of αλληλεγγύη. It is by opening towards what is considered as external that the defining perimeters are questioned and shifted and the perimeter's pores are being enlarged, rearranged, and reshaped.

The necessary porosity of commoning

This is where the idea of the threshold becomes important both as part of an interpretative effort and as part of an emerging spatial politics of emancipatory commoning. We have seen in the cases explored in this book that spaces of commoning were actualized not as bounded places but as areas with porous boundaries. The Zapatista territory, the Bon Pastor, and La Polvorilla neighborhoods, the occupied spaces of the squares movement and the alternative learning space developed out of an arrangement of collectively constructed chairs, are all spaces that communicate with their outside. The degree and the conditions of the permeability of such porous spaces vary, of course. However, what they share in common is the effort of those who inhabit them to create and maintain them through such interactive interfaces.

Apart from describing the spatial conditions of the corresponding commoning practices, threshold may become the image to illustrate the characteristics of expanding commoning. Returning to the problem of a commoning community's openness we can thus agree that such is a community which constructs and inhabits thresholds. It is a community that builds and develops itself and its members through a threshold mentality.

The threshold, in such a context, is more than a metaphor. A metaphor may compare and thus establish analogies between ideas and experiences, a metaphor may show through a familiar image the qualitative characteristics of an abstract idea. In our case, the threshold metaphor may help us understand a form of distinction between two entities that get involved in a relation of externality (or, to be more precise, in a relation of difference,

which, due to closeness, to propinquity, is perceived as externality): a community and its "outside."

Threshold, considered as a thought image (a *Denkbild*), is a
metaphor that is being explored as a source of knowledge and
reflective thinking. Once the metaphoric comparison is established, one can further build thought chains that extend the
meaning of the comparison. Once openness is characterized
as threshold-like we are urged to explore those elements of the
image that may help us understand the workings of this kind of
openness. What makes a threshold function as a threshold? What
kind of mechanisms generate, regulate, and guarantee the passage
from one side to another? What does it mean to envisage openness as a regulated passage? As a dynamic process of developing
porosity?

As we have seen, specific spatial arrangements may concretize
the functions of the threshold. From the loosely defined symbolic
borders of Zapatista territory in Oventic to the explicitly marked
entrances of La Polvorilla (which, however, are more like symbolic
markers than check-points) a whole range of threshold definitions
for common space becomes possible. From such concretizations
productive thoughts about the defining qualities of commoning
may emerge. Zapatistas build their autonomy project by creating
thresholds within a society. Through those thresholds they communicate with all those who suffer and resist, without trying to
include them in an all-encompassing project that they themselves
will lead. The University of Workers at IMPA is a threshold-
creating educational initiative which opens to the different needs
of workers, neighbors, and activists. The Rietveld chairs (produced by an open community of solidarity) both symbolized and
made possible this threshold education. Participation of future
inhabitants in planning and design of housing areas (and, in the
case of USINA projects, during their construction) is an activity
which perforates through communicating thresholds the erected
barriers between expert knowledge and popular wisdom, between
different cultural pre-dispositions, and between differing social
experiences.

Thresholds, thus, mark the actual processes through which the
common ground that is necessary for commoning practices to

develop is actually produced or discovered. By regulating and activating passages, the potentiality of common ground is explored.
Common ground emerges as the product of such crossings from
one side of the threshold to the other. Common ground does not
pre-exist commoning, it is being created through commoning.

Throughout the book various descriptive terms connected to
the spatial experience of thresholds have been used: pore, passage,
bridge, crossing (and crossroads), intermediary zone. In the use
of these terms, specific qualitative characteristics of thresholds
were called upon: porosity, in-betweenness, osmosis, transition.
Obviously this is not simply a use of synonyms. One can indeed
trace in the richness of the descriptive term threshold an equal
richness of its metaphoric uses: interestingly all those uses never
depart from initial spatial images connected to recognizable experiences in space. It seems that societies need to apprehend and
symbolize change by using familiar images based on the experience of crossing space. No matter how abstract the idea of in-
betweenness becomes in an argument, the spatial root is vividly
present.

Thus, in connecting the idea of expanding commoning (considered as a potentially emancipating process) to the image of
threshold-crossing, a lot more than a useful illustration is generated. In this gesture we realize that we can never really depart
from actual experiences of space when we try to envisage the
emancipating potential of commoning. It is in space but also
through the exploration of spatial qualities that we may activate this potential. This is another way of boldly affirming that
space matters for social emancipation, not only because social
life unfolds in space but because social life can be examined and
dreamed upon through images of spaces: lived spaces, possible
spaces, ambiguous spaces lingering between reality and fiction,
between concreteness and abstractness, between familiarity and
surprise.

The potentiality of common ground is both the result and the
prospect of threshold building. The potentialization of space,
and the potentialization of social relations are processes that
develop through thresholds. The dynamics of commoning per-
forate enclosures and potentialize passages. Beyond the prevalent

immunitarian paradigm, thresholds, social pores, breathe in solidarity.

Spatialities of emancipation?

An important part of the book's argument is based on the distinction between different forms of spatiality through which contemporary urban form and experience is shaped. The distinction between the territory, the house (and housing), and the object (as a generator of spatial arrangements), defines possible levels of spatial organization in which inhabited space is potentialized through commoning. This spatial typology proved to be more than a heuristic classification. The different ways of spatial potentialization challenge a major imposed categorization that controls the uses and symbolization of space: public versus private. Observing the dynamics of commoning in territory, housing, and object arrangements, we may actually trace the ways that common space emerges as distinct from public and private space. In the seemingly loosely defined area of the inhabited territory, lines of control (borders of a different kind) organize a network of space-embedded regulations. The public may be reduced to the state-controlled or identified with a closed communal area. Commoning as a force that challenges enclosure may convert the territory to an arrangement of thresholds. Autonomy, thus, may not be confined to the barricaded stronghold of a "liberated territory" but may be spatialized as an expanding, metastatic project of porous commoning spaces. This was actually the dynamics of the squares movement, which was confronted by the suffocating enclosing attacks of autarchic mechanisms.

In housing areas, and especially in settlements developed to house those who cannot themselves satisfy their need for a decent shelter, we may observe a different dynamics. The conditions of living together and the inventiveness enhanced by the lack of adequate means to live a life worthy of its meaning, make people overspill the boundaries that separate the private space of the apartment and the public space of the neighborhood or the settlement. Aided, as seen in many cases, by militant experts, people produce, through their participation, potentialities but also actual experiences of space-commoning. By sometimes transcending existing regulations of use (based on strict property definitions) or by shaping regulations of shared appropriation through the establishment of common property (as in the autonomous neighborhoods in Mexico or the FUCVAM housing cooperatives in Uruguay), inhabitants produce common spaces in which life is based on collective inventiveness and collaboration. In reminiscence of Walter Benjamin's and Asja Lacis' text on Naples, in such cases, "the house is far less the refuge into which people retreat than the inexhaustible reservoir from which they flood out" (Benjamin 1985b: 174).

Urban porosity and the threshold spatiality of commoning (Stavrides 2018), thus, recast architectural design problems connected to housing. Questioning the limits and symbolizations of public space, challenging the power relations that produce public space – considered as the space controlled by a certain authority – has generated interesting experiments of common space production in housing areas. If in territories the spatiality of thresholds perforates the controlling regulations of public space enclosures, in housing-as-common it is both the private and the public realm that are being re-defined and reshaped.

We can say that in such practices of habitation, relations of sharing space and of sharing through space carry in them the potentialities of emancipating processes. It is important to see the autonomous territories and the autonomous neighborhoods not as liberated or emancipated areas of a certain society but as catalysts of emancipating acts and experiences. This is the way that we can trace prefigurative elements in shared life as it unfolds in them.

What is it, then, that today makes the practices of commoning not only urgently needed for the everyday survival of those who are increasingly deprived of the necessary means for a decent life but also capable of prefiguring an emancipating society? Maybe it is the fact that commoning can support different forms of social organization: if in such forms solidarity becomes a force that ensures equality then commoning develops as an emancipating process. In place of finished plans for an emancipatory future let us try to learn from acts of real existing people how to develop commoning experiences that gesture towards a myriad possible emancipating futures. And if space may play a role in such experiences, it is space understood and lived not as the locus of closed communities and identities but as the potentializing arrangement of interconnected thresholds. Autonomy is by no means an "immunitarian" project for the "chosen ones" but an ever expanding inclusive project that feeds from collective inventiveness and from struggles against crippling enclosures.

References

Abellán, J., Sequera, J., and Janoschka, M. (2012). 'Occupying the #Hotelmadrid: a laboratory for urban resistance.' *Social Movement Studies*, vol. 11/3–4, 320–326.

Agamben, G. (1993). *The Coming Community* (Minneapolis, MN: University of Minnesota Press).

Agamben, G. (2000). 'Form of life.' In *Means Without End* (Minneapolis, MN: University of Minnesota Press), 3–12.

Agamben, G. (2007). 'The work of man.' In M. Calarco and S. Decaroli (eds), *Giorgio Agamben: Sovereignty and Life* (Stanford, CA: Stanford University Press), 1–10.

Agamben, G. (2014). 'What is destituent power?' *Environment and Planning D: Society and Space*, vol. 32, 65–74.

Alexander, J. C. (2011). *Performative Revolution in Egypt: An Essay in Cultural Power* (New York: Bloomsbury Academic).

Arantes, P. (2004). 'Reinventing the building site.' In *Brazilian Architecture in the XXth century* (London: Phaidon) vol. 1, 170–210.

Arantes, P. (2013). 'Red São Paulo in the 1980s: Workers Party, grassroots movements, experimental architecture and current impasses,' *Symposium on Architecture and the City: The Vicissitudes of Participation*. Leuven on 3–4 May 2013. Available at https://www.academia.edu/35591380/Red_S%C3%A3o_Paulo_in_the_1980s_Workers_Party_grassroots_movements_experimental_architecture_and_current_impasses, accessed 17 December 2018.

Atkinson, R. and Blandy, S. (2005). 'Introduction: international perspectives on the new enclavism and the rise of gated communities,' *Housing Studies*, vol. 20/2, 177–86.

Atkinson, R. and Blandy, S. (2017). *Domestic Fortress: Fear and the New Home Front* (Manchester: Manchester University Press).

Barrington-Bush, L. (2016). 'Defeating fear: lessons from Mexico's housing movement'. Available at https://roarmag.org/essays/defeating-fear-lessons-mexicos-housing-movement/, accessed 26 November 2018.

Baudrillard, J. (1983). *Simulations* (New York: Semiotext(e)).

Bellinghausen, H. (2004). 'Homero no debió de morir,' *La Jornada Semanal*, 22 August, no. 494, 7.

Benjamin W. (1983). *Charles Baudelaire: A Lyric Poet in the Era of High Capitalism* (London: Verso).

Benjamin, W. (1985a). 'Moscow.' In *One Way Street and Other Writings* (London: Verso), 177–207.

Benjamin, W. (1985b). 'Naples.' In *One Way Street and Other Writings* (London: Verso), 167–176.

Benjamin, W. (1992a). 'Theses on the philosophy of history.' In *Illuminations* (London: Fontana Press), 245–255.

Benjamin, W. (1992b). 'The task of the translator.' In *Illuminations* (London: Fontana Press), 70–82.

Benjamin, W. (1999). *The Arcades Project* (Cambridge, MA: The Belknap Press).

Blau, E. (1999). *The Architecture of Red Vienna, 1919–1934* (Cambridge, MA: MIT Press).

Bourdieu, P. (1977). *Outline of a Theory of Practice* (Cambridge: Cambridge University Press).

Bourdieu, P. (1991). *Language and Symbolic Power* (Cambridge: Polity Press).

Bourdieu, P. (2000). *Pascalian Meditations* (Cambridge: Polity Press).

Breines, W. (1982). *The Great Refusal: Community and Organization in the New Left: 1962–1968* (New York: Praeger).

Brighenti, A. M. (2010). 'On territorology: towards a general science of territory,' *Theory, Culture & Society*, vol. 27/1, 52–72.

Brown, N. (2013). 'The modality of sovereignty: Agamben and the *aporia* of primacy in Aristotle's *Metaphysics* theta', *Mosaic*, vol. 46/1, 169–182.

Caldeira, T. (2000). *City of Walls: Crime, Segregation and Citizenship in São Paulo* (Berkeley, CA: University of California Press).

Campbell, T. and Sitze, A. (2013). *Biopolitics: A Reader* (Durham NC: Duke University Press).

Castro, D., Fry, M., and Menendez, M. (2012). 'Desafios para pensar los movimientos sociales Uruguayos: FUCVAM y sus estrategias de formacion en la era progresista,' *Contrapunto*, Decembre, 33–51.

Colla, L., Peeters, C., and Preud'homme, C. (2015). *Mutirao: Collective autoconstruction in São Paulo*. Master of Science in the Ingenieurswetenschappen: architecture (Leuven: University of Leuven).

Col.Lectiu Repensar Bonpastor (eds) (2016). *Repensar Bonpastor: Teijendo historias urbanas de Barcelona desde el umbral de las Casas Baratas* (Barcelona: Col.Lectiu Repensar Bonpastor).

Colloredo-Mansfield, R. (2009). *Fighting Like a Community: Andean Civil Society in an Era of Indian Uprisings* (Chapel Hill: University of North Carolina Press).

Colquhoun, A. (1985). 'The superblock.' In *Essays in Architectural Criticism* (Cambridge, MA: MIT Press), 83–103.

Davidoff, P. (1965). 'Advocacy and pluralism in planning,' *AIP Journal* vol. 31/4, 331–338.

De Angelis, M. (2007). *The Beginning of History: Value Struggles and Global Capital* (London: Pluto).

De Angelis, M. (2017) *Omnia Sunt Communia On the Commons and the Transformation to Postcapitalism* (London: Zed Books).

De Angelis, M. and S. Stavrides (2010). 'Beyond markets or states: commoning as collective practice (a public interview)', *An Architektur*, 23 (also at www.e-flux.com/journal/view/150).

de Certeau, M. (1984). *The Practice of Everyday Life* (Minneapolis, MN: University of Minnesota Press).

Deladurantaye, L. (2000). 'Agamben's potential', *Diacritics*, vol. 30/2, 3–24.

de Man, P. (1986). *Resistance to Theory* (Minneapolis, MN: University of Minnesota Press).

Detienne, M. and Vernant, J. P. (1991). *Cunning Intelligence in Greek Culture and Society* (Chicago: Chicago University Press).

Durkheim, E. (2014). *The Division of Labor in Society* (New York: Free Press).

Elden, S. (2007). 'Governmentality, calculation, territory,' *Environment and Planning D: Society and Space*, vol. 25, 562–580.

Escobar, A. (2001). 'Culture sits in places: reflections on globalism and subaltern strategies of localization,' *Political Geography*, vol. 20, 139–174.

Esposito, R. (2006). 'Interview,' *Diacritics*, vol. 36/2, 49–56.

Esposito, R. (2010). *Communitas: The Origin and Destiny of Community* (Stanford: Stanford University Press).

Esposito, R. (2013). 'Community, immunity, biopolitics,' *Angelaki*, vol. 8/3, 83–90.

Esteva, G. (2012). 'Hope from the margins.' In D. Bollier and S. Helfrich (eds), *The Wealth of the Commons: A World beyond Market and State* (Amherst MA: Levellers Press). Available at http://wealthofthecom mons.org/essay/hope-margins, accessed 27 November 2018.

Esteva, G. (2015). 'Enclosing the enclosers: autonomous experiences from the grassroots – beyond development, globalization and post-modernity.' In F. Luisetti, J. Pickles, and W. Kaiser (eds), *The Anomie of the Earth: Philosophy, Politics, and Autonomy in Europe and the Americas* (Durham NC: Duke University Press), 71–92.

Faas, A. J. (2017). 'Enduring cooperation: time, discipline, and Minga Practice in disaster-induced displacement and resettle-ment in the Ecuadorian Andes,' *Human Organization*, vol. 76/2, 99–108.

Fathy, H. (1973). *Architecture for the Poor* (Chicago: Chicago University Press).

Fernández-Savater, A. and Flesher Fominaya, C. (eds), with contribu-tions by Luhuna Carvalho, Çiğdem, Hoda Elsadda, Wiam El-Tamami, Patricia Horrillo, Silvia Nanclares & Stavros Stavrides (2017). 'Life after the squares: reflections on the consequences of the Occupy movements,' *Social Movement Studies*, 16/1, 119–151.

Ferro, S. (2015). '"Trabahador coletivo" e autonomia.' In Icaro Vilaca and Paula Constante (eds), *USINA: Entre o Projeto e o Canteiro* (São Paulo: Aurora).

Ferro, S. (2016). 'Dessin/chantier. an introduction.' In Katie L. Thomas, Tilo Amhoft, and Nick Beech (eds), *Industries of Architecture* (New York: Routledge), 95–105.

Foucault, M. (1997). 'The ethics of the concern of the self as a practice of freedom.' In P. Rabinow (ed.), *Michel Foucault: Ethics, Subjectivity and Truth* (New York: The New Press, 281–301).

Foucault, M. (2000). 'Space, knowledge and power.' In James D. Faubion (ed.), *Power: The Essential Works of Foucault, 1954–1984*, vol. 3 (New York: The New Press), 349–364.

Foucault, M. (2009). *Security, Territory, Population* (New York: Palgrave Macmillan).

Freire, P. (2005). *Pedagogy of the Oppressed* (London: Continuum).

Giovanopoulos, C. and Mitropoulos, D. (2011). *Democracy Under Construction* (in Greek) (Athens: Asynecheia).

Hardt, M. and Negri, A. (2005). *Multitude: War and Democracy in the Age of Empire* (London: Hamish Hamilton).

Hardt, M. and A. Negri (2009). *Commonwealth* (Cambridge, MA: Harvard University Press).

Harvey, D. (2012). *Rebel Cities: From the Right to the City to the Urban Revolution* (London: Verso).

Hénaff, M. and Strong, T. (eds) (2001). *Public Space and Democracy* (Minneapolis, MN: University of Minnesota Press).

Heynen, H. (1999). *Architecture and Modernity: A Critique* (Cambridge, MA: MIT Press).

Higuchi, F., Lazarini, K. and Barbosa, S. (2015). 'USINA 25 anos – Mutirões Tânia Maria e Cinco de Dezembro.' *Archdaily*. Available at https://www.archdaily.com.br/br/768645/usina-25-anos-mutiroes-tania-maria-e-cinco-de-dezembro, accessed 17 November 2017.

Holloway, J. (2002). *Change the World Without Taking Power* (London: Pluto Press).

Holloway, J. (2010). *Crack Capitalism* (London: Pluto Press).

Holston, J. (1991). 'Autoconstruction in working-class Brazil,' *Cultural Anthropology*, vol. 6/4 (November 1991), 447–465.

Holston, J. (2008). *Insurgent Citizenship: Disjunctions of Democracy and Modernity in Brazil* (Princeton, NJ: Princeton University Press).

Hotel Madrid (2011). 'Nuevo espacio liberado: Hotel Madrid en la calle Carretas.' Available at https://madrid.tomalaplaza.net/2011/10/16/nuevo-espacio-liberado-hotel-madrid-en-la-calle-carretas/, accessed 17 December 2018.

Juarez-Galeana, L. G. (2006). 'Collaborative public open space design in self-help housing: Minas-Polvorilla, Mexico City.' In Roger Zetter and Georgia Butina Watson (eds), *Designing Sustainable Cities in the Developing World* (Aldershot: Ashgate), 179–196.

Karasulu, A. (2015). '"We may be lessees but the neighbouhood is ours." Gezi Resistance and Spatial Claims.' In I. David and K. Toktamus (eds), *'Everywhere Taksim': Sowing the Seeds for a New Turkey at Gezi* (Amsterdam: Amsterdam University Press), 201–214.

Kwinter, S. (2002). *Architectures of Time: Toward a Theory of the Event in Modernist Culture* (Cambridge: MIT Press).

Laclau, E. (1996). *Emancipation(s)* (London: Verso).

Lazar, S. (2008). *El Alto, Rebel City: Self and Citizenship in Andean Bolivia* (Durham NC: Duke University Press).

Le Corbusier (1987). *The City of To-morrow and its Planning* (New York: Dover Publication).

Lefebvre, H. (1991). *The Production of Space* (Oxford: Blackwell).

Lefebvre, H. (1996). *Writings on Cities* (Oxford: Blackwell).

Lefebvre, H. (2009). *State, Space, World: Selected essays* (Minneapolis, MN: University of Minnesota Press).

Lemke, T. (2011). *Biopolitics: An Advanced Introduction* (New York: New York University Press).

Leontidou, L. (1990). *The Mediterranean City in Transition: Social Change and Urban Development* (Cambridge: Cambridge University Press).

Letseka, Moeketsi (2014). 'Ubuntu and justice as fairness,' *Mediterranean Journal of Social Sciences*, vol. 5/9, 544–551.

Linebaugh, P. (2008). *The Magna Carta Manifesto* (Berkeley, CA: University of California Press).

Lyotard, J. F. (1993). 'On the strength of the weak.' In J. F. Lyotard, *Toward the Postmodern* (Atlantic Highlands, NJ: Humanities Press), 62–72.

Máčel, O., S. Woertman, and C. Van Wijk (2008). *Chairs: The Delft Collection* (Rotterdam: OIO Publishers).

Machado, G. (2016). 'La experiencia de las cooperativas de vivienda en Uruguay: necesidades, organizacion e imaginacion,' *Vivienda Popular*, vol. 28, 32–39.

Maricato, E. (2009). 'Fighting for just cities in capitalism's periphery.' In P. Marcuse, J. Connoly, J. Novy, I. Olivo, C. Potter, and J. Steil (eds), *Searching for the Just City: Debates in Urban Theory and Practice* (London: Routledge), 72–88.

Maricato, E. (2016). 'The recent urban protests in Brazil.' Available at https://erminiamaricato.net/2016/07/17/the-recent-urban-protests-in-brazil/, accessed 20 July 2017.

Mezzadra, S. and Neilson, B. (2013). *Border as Method, or the Multiplication of Method* (Durham NC: Duke University Press).

Miller Lane, B. (1985). *Architecture and Politics in Germany 1918–1945* (Cambridge, MA: Harvard University Press).

Minton, A. (2009). *Ground Control: Fear and Happiness in the Twenty-First-Century City* (London: Penguin Books).

Minton, A. (2015). 'Byker Wall: Newcastle's noble failure of an estate – A history of cities in 50 buildings,' *The Guardian*. Available at www.theguardian.com/cities/2015/may/21/byker-wall-newcastles-noble-failure-of-an-estate-a-history-of-cities-in-50-buildings-day-41, accessed 26 November 2018.

Nadal-Melsió, S. (2008). 'Lessons in surrealism: relationality, event, encounter.' In K. Goonewardena, S. Kipfer, R. Milgrom, and C. Schmid (eds), *Space, Difference, Everyday Life: Reading Henri Lefebvre* (New York: Routledge), 161–175.

Nahoum, B. (2013). *Algunas Claves: Reflexiones sobre Aspectos Esenciales de la Vivienda Cooperativa por Ayuda Mutua* (Montevideo: Trilce).

Nahoum, B. (2015). 'El Movimiento Cooperativista del Uruguay: autogestion, ayuda mutua, aporte proprio, propiedad collectiva.' In A. del Castillo and R. Valles (eds), *Cooperativas de Vivienda en Uruguay* (Montevideo: Facultad de Architectura, Universidad de la Republica), 36–47.

Nancy, J. L. (1991). 'Of being in common.' In Miami Theory Collective (eds), *Community at Loose Ends* (Minneapolis, MN: University of Minnesota Press), 1–12.

Nancy, J. L. (2000). *Being Singular Plural* (Stanford CA: Stanford University Press).

Nancy, J. L. (2010). 'Communism, the word (notes for the conference).' In C. Douzinas and S. Žižek (eds), *The Idea of Communism* (London: Verso), 145–153.

Olsson, J. (ed.), (2011). *El Camino Posible: Produccion del Habitat en America Latina* (Montevideo: Trilce).

One School for Chiapas Greek Solidarity Group (2004). 'Breve bitacora de una escuela en la selva,' *La Jornada Semanal*, 22 August 2004, no. 494, 4–5.

Pessina, L. (2016). 'Cicuenta anos de cooperativismopor ayuda mutua: mis cooperativas, mi vida,' *Vivienda Popular*, vol. 28, 14–23.

Porto-Gonçalves, C. W. and Leff, E. (2015). 'Political ecology in Latin America: the social re-appropriation of nature, the reinvention of territories and the construction of an environmental rationality,' *Desenvolvimento e Meio Ambiente*, vol. 35, 65–88.

Progressive Architecture (1968). Advocacy planning: how it is, how it works, *Progressive Architecture* (September), 102–115.

Raffestin, Cl. (2012). 'Space, territory, and territoriality,' *Environment and Planning D: Society and Space*, vol. 30, 121–141.

Rancière, J. (2006). *The Politics of Aesthetics* (London: Continuum).

Rancière, J. (2009). *The Emancipated Spectator* (London: Verso).

Rancière, J. (2010). *Dissensus: On Politics and Aesthetics* (London: Continuum).

Rancière, J. (2013). *Aisthesis: Scenes from the Aesthetic Regime of Art* (London: Verso).

Rancière, J. (2017). 'Art, life, finality: the metamorphoses of beauty,' *Critical Inquiry* vol. 43 (Spring), 598–616.

Reyes, A. and Kaufman, M. (2011). 'Sovereignty, indigeneity, territory: Zapatista autonomy and the new practices of decolonization,' *The South Atlantic Quarterly* vol. 110/2, 505–525.

Reyes, A. (2015). 'Zapatismo: other geographies circa "the end of the world",' *Environment and Planning D: Society and Space*, vol. 33, 408–424.

Richter, G. (2007). *Thought-Images: Frankfurt School Writers' Reflections from Damaged Life* (Stanford, CA: Stanford University Press).

Rivas Alonso, C. (2015). 'Gezi Park. a revindication of public space.' In I. David and K. Toktamus (eds), *'Everywhere Taksim': Sowing the Seeds for a New Turkey at Gezi* (Amsterdam: Amsterdam University Press), 231–247.

Roggero, G. (2010). 'Five theses on the common,' *Rethinking Marxism*, vol. 22/3, 357–373.

Ruggeri, A. and Vieta, M. (2015). 'Argentina's worker-recuperated enterprises, 2010–2013: a synthesis of recent empirical findings,' *Journal of Entrerpreneurial and Organizational Diversity*, vol. 4/1, 75–103.

Santos Carvalho, C. and Rossbach, A. (2010). *The City Statute: A commentary* (São Paulo: Cities Alliance and Ministry of Cities).

Sassen, S. (2006). *Territory, Authority, Rights: From Medieval to Global Assemblages* (Princeton: Princeton University Press).

Sassen, S. (2014). *Expulsion: Brutality and Complexity in the Global Economy* (Cambridge, MA: The Belknap Press).

Scanlon, K. and Whitehead, C. (eds) (2008) *Social Housing in Europe II: A Review of Policies and Outcomes* (London: LSE).

Schwartz, A. (2006). Housing policy in the United States (New York: Routledge).

Schechner, R. (1985). *Between Theater and Anthropology* (Philadelphia: University of Pennsylvania Press).

Scott, J. (2009). *The Art of not Being Governed* (New Haven: Yale University Press).

Segawa, H. (2013). *Architecture of Brazil 1900–1960* (New York: Springer).

Sennett, R. (1994). *Flesh and Stone: The Body and the City in Western Civilization* (London: Faber and Faber).

Shulman, A. (2012). 'The fifty days of the Hotel Madrid.' Available at https://lareviewofbooks.org/article/the-fifty-days-of-the-hotel-madrid /#!, accessed 17 December 2018.

Sitrin, M. (2006). *Horizontalism: Voices of Popular Power in Argentina* (Oakland: AK Press).

Sontag, S. (1978). *Illness as Metaphor* (New York: Farrar, Straus and Giroux).

Sontag, S. (1989). *AIDS and its Metaphors* (New York: Farrar, Straus and Giroux).

Stavrides, S. (2010). *Towards the City of Thresholds* (Trento: Professionaldreamers).

Stavrides, S. (2014). 'Emerging common spaces as a challenge to the city of crisis, *CITY*, vol. 18/4–5, 546–550.

Stavrides, S. (2016). *Common Space: The City as Commons* (London: Zed Books).

Stavrides, S. (2018). 'Urban porosity and the right to a shared city.' In S. Wolfrum, H. Stengel, F. Kurbasik, N. Kling, S. Dona, I. Mumm, and C. Zoehrer (eds), *Porous City: From Metaphor to Agenda* (Basel: Birkhauser), 32–37.

Stavrides, S., Kopanari, M., Koutrolikou P., Marathou C., Vatavali F., and Guizeli, V. (2009). *Transformations of the Relation between Public and Private Space in Greek Social Housing Complexes* (Unpublished Research Project funded by NTUA).

Steele, J. (1988). *Hasan Fathy*. Architectural Monographs (London: Academy Editions).

Stollmann, J. (2014). 'The academy for a new gropiusstadt: productive common spaces.' In Francesca Ferguson (ed.), *Make-Shift City: Renegotiating the Urban Commons* (Berlin: Jovis Verlag), 134–135.

Swanson, D. (2007). 'Ubuntu: an African contribution to (re)search for/with a "humble togetherness",' *Journal of Contemporary Issues in Education*, vol. 2/2, 53–67.

Tafuri, M. (1990). *The Sphere and the Labyrinth: Avant-gardes and Architecture from Piranesi to the 1970s* (Cambridge, MA: MIT Press).

Thompson, E. P. (1993). *Customs in Common* (New York: The New Press).

Thorburn, E. (2017). 'Realising the common: the assembly as an organising structure.' In G. Ruivenkamp and A. Hilton (eds), *Perspectives on Commoning: Autonomist Principles and Practices* (London: Zed Books), 65–106.

Turner, V. (1986). 'Dewey, Dilthey, and drama: an essay in the anthropology of experience.' In V. Turner and E. Bruner (eds), *The Anthropology of Experience* (Chicago: University of Illinois Press), 33–44.

UN Habitat (2004). 'Architecture and urban design including landscape and cultural recovery in the housing project "Minas Polvorilla".' Available at http://mirror.unhabitat.org/bp/bp.list.details.aspx?bp_id=501, accessed 26 November 2018.

USINA (2006). 'Self administered vertical habitation for densely populated urban conditions: Copromo, União da Juta e Paulo Freire Projects, Brazil.' In BSHF Report (December 2006). Available at http://courses.arch.ntua.gr/fsr/134924/BSHF_Final_Usina_Brasil.pdf, accessed 25 September 2014.

USINA (2015). 'Processos de projeto como construção de autonomia.' In I. Vilaca and P. Constante (eds) *USINA: Entre o Projeto e o Canteiro* (São Paulo: Aurora), 155–167.

Van de Sande, M. (2013). 'The prefigurative politics of Tahrir Square – an alternative perspective on the 2011 Revolutions', *Res Publica*, vol. 19, 223–239.

Van de Sande, M. (2017). 'The prefigurative power of the common(s).' In G. Ruivenkamp and A. Hilton (eds) *Perspectives on Commoning* (London: Zed books), 25–63.

Van Zijl, I. and Kuper M. (1992). *Rietveld Gerrit: The Complete Works 1888–1964* (Utrecht: Centraal Museum).

Velázquez, E. T. (2014). 'A Pancho Villa no lo enterramos, lo sembramos. FPFVI-UNOPII, Comunidad de comunidades en la Ciudad de México.' El Canelado de la Ciudad (Facultad Latinoamericana de Ciencias Sociales (FLACSO) en Ecuador), no. 3, 100–111.

Vernant, J. P. (2006). *Myth and Thought Among the Greeks* (New York: Zone Books).

Vieta, M. (2014). 'Learning in struggle: Argentina's new worker cooperatives as transformative learning organizations.' *Relations Industrielles/ Industrial Relations*, vol. 69/1, 186–218.

Virno, P. (2004). *A Grammar of the Multitude* (New York: Semiotext(e)).

Virno, P. (2008). *Multitude: Between Innovation and Negation* (Los Angeles: Semiotext(e)).

Virno, P. (2009). 'Anthropology and theory of institutions.' In G. Rannig and G. Ray (eds), *Art and Contemporary Critical Practice: Reinventing Institutional Critique* (London: MayFly Books), 95–112.

Virno, P. (2015a). *Déjà vu and the End of History* (London: Verso).

Virno, P. (2015b). *When the Word Becomes Flesh: Language and Human Nature* (Los Angeles: Semiotext(e)).

Wacquant, L. (2008). *Urban Outcasts* (Cambridge: Polity Press).

Weigel, S. (1996). *Body- and Image-Space: Re-reading Walter Benjamin* (London: Routledge).

White, M. (2003). *De Stijl and Dutch Modernism* (Manchester: Manchester University Press).

Wilmer, S. E. and Žukauskaite, A. (2016) *Resisting Biopolitics: Philosophical, Political, and Performative Strategies* (New York: Routledge).

Zibechi, R. (2007). *Autonomías y emancipaciones: América Latina en movimiento* (Lima: Programa Democracia y Transformación Global and Fondo Editorial de la Facultad de Ciencias Sociales, Unidad de Post Grado, UNMSM).

Zibechi, R. (2010). *Dispersing Power: Social Movements as Anti-State Forces* (Oakland: AK Press).

Zibechi, R. (2012). *Territories in Resistance: A Cartography of Latin American Movements* (Oakland: AK Press).

Zibechi, R. (2014). 'Mexico: challenges and difficulties of urban territories in resistance.' In R. Stahler-Sholk, H. E. Vanden, and M. Becker (eds), *Rethinking Latin American Social Movements* (Lanham: Rowman and Littlefield), 49–65.

Zito Lema, A. and Blaton, N. (2012). *Sitting is a Verb: Rietveld for IMPA* (Anthropologists in Art and Proconsul Editions).

Index

EU authorised representative for GPSR:
Easy Access System Europe, Mustamäe tee 50,
10621 Tallinn, Estonia
gpsr.requests@easproject.com

www.ingramcontent.com/pod-product-compliance
Lightning Source LLC
Chambersburg PA
CBHW050642280326
41932CB00015B/2749